Judith Spelman is a journalist and author who was involved in setting up the Stamford Book Festival and Oundle Festival of Literature. She started the Sherborne Literary Festival and ran it for four years before stepping down to spend time on her writing. She has learnt from experience how to make a festival work and has spoken to numerous festival organisers about the way they run their festivals.

OTHER TITLES

How to Be Confident and Assertive at Work
The Pocket Media Coach
Quick Wins in Sales and Marketing
How to Manage Difficult People
Planning and Managing a Corporate Event
Management Starts with You
Stand, Speak, Deliver!

The Festival Organiser's Bible

How to Plan, Organise and Run a Successful Festival

Judith Spelman

ROBINSON

ROBINSON

First published in Great Britain in 2018 by Robinson

Copyright © Judith Spelman, 2018
Appendix II text copyright © the Society of Authors, 2016

1 3 5 7 9 10 8 6 4 2

The moral right of the author has been asserted.

A CIP catalogue record for this book is available from the British Library

ISBN: 978-1-47213-908-5

Typeset in New Caledonia LT by Hewer Text UK Ltd, Edinburgh
Printed and bound in Great Britain by CPI Group (UK), Croydon CR0 4YY

Papers used by Robinson are from well-managed
forests and other responsible sources

Robinson
An imprint of
Little, Brown Book Group
Carmelite House
50 Victoria Embankment
London EC4Y 0DZ

An Hachette UK Company
www.hachette.co.uk

www.littlebrown.co.uk

Contents

Preface

Organising a festival can be exciting, stimulating and rewarding, providing you plan carefully and ensure that basic principles are firmly in place. This applies to all festivals – literary, music, food, folk, arts – no matter how large or how small.

Certain decisions have to be made at the beginning to ensure success. This book explains why you need to choose people to work with carefully; the importance of commitment; why it is vital to get the timing right; ways to make your festival unique and problems that may occur and how to deal with them. You will discover how to raise money to cover initial costs, find sponsors, learn about the benefits of building a working relationship with agents and publishers and ways of compiling a balanced programme. You will get an understanding of marketing, publicity and advertising, and liaising with local media.

There's no better way of finding out what makes a good festival than hearing some of the experiences – good and bad – of authors, musicians and stallholders and organisers. Organisers of a variety of festivals explain how they prepare and give advice based on what they have learnt. You will read valuable tips from some of our top festival directors – including Michael Eavis (Glastonbury Festival), Kenneth Richardson (Oundle International Festival), Tanya Bruce-Lockhart (Bridport Festival) and Paul Kelly (Bournemouth Jazz

Festival). I'll also tell you about my own experience initiating the Sherborne Literary Festival and running it for four years.

Festivals are getting bigger, with more than fourteen million adults planning to visit one or more each year as of 2015. Yet there is still room for more. This book deals not only with starting a festival but also running and improving it. Whether your festival is large or small there are guidelines to put in place to make sure it is successful.

Raising money for charity, good causes and local projects can be great fun but phenomenally hard work and yet new festivals spring up every year. Is your festival the next? This book will give you the help you need to get started – or, if you have, how you can make it better.

Why start a festival?

The dictionary defines a festival as a day or period set aside for celebration or feasting, any occasion for celebration or an organised series of special events and performances. It is the latter definition that has been enthusiastically embraced in recent times by many groups and organisations. You don't have to go far to find a festival of some kind. But it wasn't always like this. There was a time when there were few festivals; villages might hold flower festivals and large towns boasted music festivals but there was little else to excite or enthral the local population.

Today it's a different story. Festivals are springing up all over the country. Not only literary festivals – beloved of authors and publishers as another way of selling books – but history festivals, cheese festivals, beer festivals, music festivals, food festivals, flower festivals, jazz festivals, arts festivals, folk festivals . . . Some are quite specific in what they offer, such as scarecrow, chilli or cheese festivals. Others create unlikely combinations such as music and food or food and vintage cars . . . food seems to feature a lot.

There are over 340 literary festivals in the UK alone and almost four hundred various types of music festivals. If you add every other type appearing regularly, there must be some sort of festival in every town or village. Yet there is still room for more – for yours. The key is to make *your* festival different. For example, the River Cottage Festival in Axminster offers music and food and Tim Barford's vegan festivals in Bristol, Brighton, London Olympia and Glasgow appear under the name Vegfest.

So, it seems a festival can offer almost anything. It can be a boutique offering in a small town or village (such as the Cheese Festival in Sturminster Newton) or a huge, all-embracing number such as those in Cheltenham, Oxford, Glastonbury and Edinburgh. But be aware, it is worth noting that as fast as one event springs up, another one fails. The question is, why? There are many answers; lack of interest from the potential audience, lack of commitment from the organisers, shaky finances, no suitable venues, bad timing, poor planning, competition or conflicts of interest.

This book takes a cross-section of many different festivals and finds out why they work, what problems have been overcome or, where they haven't, why they have failed. It offers sensible guidelines for setting up and running a festival, and if you need more advice then contact the Association of Festival Organisers (www.festivalorganisers.org) whose general secretary, Steve Heap, is very helpful.

1

Planning a festival

People hold festivals for many different reasons, including location, history, facilities and the passions of the organisers. Often it is a combination of all of these factors.

REASONS TO RUN A FESTIVAL

People often feel daunted or nervous at the idea of running a festival. They think of the festivals they have visited, the size of them, the different things that are happening, the people. They think of the big beasts – Hay-on-Wye, Ways with Words, Cheltenham, Glastonbury. What they don't think about is the *beginnings* of these festivals. These events didn't just spring up fully formed. They began in a small way and over the years have improved and grown, through the hard work and inspiration of their organisers. The main points to remember are:

- Start small
- Don't be too ambitious
- Choose a theme that you understand – and love

Even the smallest festival can make enough money to expand and donate to charity. Take the Bridport Hat Festival that runs for a couple of days in early September. It was started in 2010 by Roger Snook, whose family millinery business has served the town since 1896. When he took over in 1987 they were a gentlemen's outfitters but he decided to build up the hat side, providing unusual headwear for films and television. The Hat Festival followed and from the beginning it was a huge success with the quirkiness of the idea providing international appeal.

HOW QUIRKY IDEAS CAN BE DEVELOPED INTO A SUCCESSFUL FESTIVAL

Hats off

The first Hat Festival began in 2010 and by 2016 more than 14,000 people visited Bridport, celebrating hats by wearing incredible creations on their heads. Money raised goes to Brain Tumour Research and the Brain Injury Rehabilitation Trust.

Raising money for the church

The Revd Michael Anderson wanted to raise money for the sixteen parishes administered by the Three Valleys Team Benefice in Yetminster. He devised a week-long festival with a variety of events culminating in a performance by the London Symphony Orchestra of Mozart's *Requiem* by candlelight. Leading up to this were events including a barn dance, a hymn quiz and lunches hosted in private houses. Anderson raised £4,000.

OUT OF PASSION

If you have a lifelong interest in something – be it needle-work, classic cars, books, photography or a hobby – you might consider holding a festival to share this with fellow enthusiasts. You can arrange a one-day festival to begin with and take it from there.

Organic farming

Luke Hasell of Valley Fest had a number of reasons to start his event. 'Valley Fest is all about promoting organic farming to everyone of all ages, everywhere in the country,' he says, 'and about re-engaging people with where their food comes from. Since I inherited the farm I've always wanted to get people onto the farm, seeing our animals and learning about how they should source their food locally and organically. We've also got Riverford, Tideford and Yeo Valley on board to help us spread that message – pioneers in the same ethos!'

> Before you launch, think of all the angles that make it work and those that could spell disaster. Be prepared to spend at least a year planning your first festival. The next will take much less time.

Raising money for the village

'We started the festival eleven years ago,' says Elizabeth Turnbull of Leigh Food Festival. 'The people in the village and the church wanted to have a flower festival and I happened to be the secretary of the fabric fund. So they asked me if I would do something. There was a committee then but that

3

was disbanded. When we started there were very few food festivals around although there are many more now. It started quite small but it became very popular, although I don't know why because this is a tiny little village. There were probably only about eighteen stalls at the beginning and now there are nearer thirty. We usually have nearly a thousand people visiting the festival, especially if the weather is good. Our annual food festival is my baby! I love doing it and I get a massive buzz out of it even though it's quite hard work.'

There is a good mixture of foods with coffee roasted locally, artisan cheese makers, cakes, gourmet soups and seafood dishes, chocolate, chilli sauces, honey, vegetarian and vegan food and unusual herbs and spices. The majority of these are local businesses.

A passion for a moral lifestyle

Tim Barford, who has won awards for his vegan festivals, is passionate about what he does. 'We believe what we do is ethical,' he says, 'and so do the people who come here. There is an environmental impact. A lot of people come here because they believe in what we are doing and a vegan lifestyle is more than just a diet, it is about taking a moral and ethical standpoint.'

Tim Barford's experience is interesting because it shows how as a festival grows it can combine other unrelated things that also interest people. Elizabeth Turnbull explains: 'We introduced a vintage vehicles show to the food festival in 2005 and that is now very popular. In 2016 we had over a hundred vintage cars and motorbikes for people to look around when they had been inside the hall to see and sample the food. I found these vintage vehicles mostly on websites and now it's just growing like Topsy. People with classic cars just love coming and visitors to the food festival love looking at them.'

All about the music

It's hard to believe that the internationally popular Glastonbury Festival has been going since 1971. It was started by Michael Eavis, who had taken on Worthy Farm after the death of his father. Michael was passionate about music and combined that with his need to diversify in order to save the family farm. 'I was in the merchant navy and my father died when I was nineteen and I had to come home,' he explains. 'I went off to sea when I was fifteen and I didn't really want to come back but I had to run the farm because I wanted to save it from being sold. I was doing it all myself and I met a girl and we went off to the Bath Blues Festival which was two miles away at the showground. It was my road to Damascus. It was wonderful!'

He decided to put on his own music festival. 'I found out I had to get a copy of *The White Book*,' he says. This is an event production directory (see www.whitebook.co.uk) that reports event news and lists event managers, entertainers, sound, lighting, staging, crew and UK venues.

Michael called his new festival The Pilton Pop, Blues and Folk Festival and tickets cost £1 – with a free bottle of milk! 'I was crazy on pop music myself,' says Michael. 'I loved Led Zeppelin. I found the Kinks for that first festival but they didn't turn up but there was some new-fangled band called T-Rex who came instead. I just gave it a go, really. I didn't know what I was doing. I built that first stage out of an old farm wagon with wooden boards on top.'

The Glastonbury Festival is now the biggest in the world. In 2016 over 200,000 people were at the four-day event.

Luke Hasell's Valley Fest takes place not that far from Glastonbury. It's a family event that takes place over a long, early September weekend in the Chew Valley near Bristol. It was started by Hasell on the family farm in Somerset as a tribute to his parents who both died tragically early. He is keen to show how important it is for the UK to feed itself without chemicals and pesticides. 'We started having a party in the valley a few years ago which we called Mini-V as a bit of a micky-take of V Festival,' explains Luke. 'Then we started Valley Fest in its current form in 2015 and it's looking even bigger in 2016 with the support of loads of the country's best organic businesses, many of whom are also based down here in the south-west!' The message is clear: follow the things you are passionate about and combine that with imagination and ingenuity.

Supporting charities

Husband and wife Nigel Ferrier and Lynda Symonds run a music festival every July in the village of Fenstanton, Cambridgeshire. It's called Fringe in the Fen. 'We give the proceeds to Macmillan Cancer Support and we decided to do this because we felt it gave the festival more purpose,' explained Lynda. 'Otherwise we would be fundraising for . . . what? Because we are raising money for Macmillan we are granted official fundraising status and that means we are able to use their public liability insurance.'

Fringe in the Fen was launched in 2011 after a lot of careful planning. 'We had the idea of a music festival simply because we are both very keen on all sorts of music and it would lend itself very well to the village,' says Lynda, who is the conference and events director, 'and we thought that we would use all the venues in the village. In 2016 we only used three venues but in previous years we used the church, a barn, Fenstanton Manor and all the greens in the village. In 2016 we had a brass band on the green and a big marquee at Fenstanton Manor where we held the prom.'

GROWING LOCAL INTERESTS

Thomas Hardy's legacy

The author and poet Thomas Hardy and the legendary author, archaeologist and diplomat T. E. Lawrence were both part of the inspiration for the Dorchester Literary Festival. 'Dorchester has a terrific literary legacy with Thomas Hardy and T. E. Lawrence and contemporary fiction writers have used us as inspiration,' says Janet Gleeson, co-director of the festival. 'As writers ourselves, my co-director Paul Atterbury, who has written over thirty books and I, having written eight books under my own name, saw a gap in the market. As we both love books and we have both been asked to speak at various festivals we thought we'd give it a try. Another reason for starting the festival is that the Dorchester museum was very eager to attract more people and a festival was another way of doing it. One of the very first people we went to see was the manager of Waterstone's bookshop because it seemed to us absolutely crucial to have a bookshop to back you up. At that meeting the manager introduced us to The Thomas Hardy Society and they are now part of the festival.'

If you are starting a festival it helps to have had well-known figures living in the area.

7

LOCAL ASSETS AND CONNECTIONS

Always take into consideration the area in which you want to hold the festival and build on its assets. For example, a bonus for the Fringe in the Fen Festival is that Lancelot 'Capability' Brown lived in the Manor House in the village and is buried in the churchyard. The four-hundredth anniversary of his birth fell in 2016 and this prompted the idea of a special event at the festival. 'We met musician Graham Ross and discussed with him our idea and what we wanted and he had contacts who were high-quality performers. We commissioned a piece of music, a violin concerto, that Graham Ross wrote and called *The Fallen Elm*,' said Lynda. 'Every time it's performed, the performing rights are donated directly to Macmillan Cancer Support. Unfortunately, the Performing Rights Society won't waive their fee and that is going to cost us eight hundred pounds. Somehow we have to raise that and we don't want to take any more money from people who have been so generous. Perhaps we could have a safari supper or teas in the garden, something like that.'

In 2016 the Fringe in the Fen Festival raised £30,000 for Macmillan Cancer Support and over the three festivals, along with other sundry fundraising events, they have raised around £130,000.

Don't begin big

James Shepard, who founded the award-winning Larmer Tree Festival, has sensible advice for a potential festival organiser. 'Start small – and get as much experience as you can at other people's festivals before you start,' he says. 'Volunteer at festivals and just get out there and learn all you can before you start your own event. Maybe put on small events in your neighbourhood and little gigs because even putting on a small event, it's amazing how much work it takes. Until you try, you don't realise how much effort actually goes into putting on an event that actually starts on time and where everybody gets paid!'

FOOD FOR THOUGHT

Food is popular. River Cottage in the south-west is known for its commitment to seasonal and ethically produced food. Established by Hugh Fearnley-Whittingstall, it has a cookery school, runs dining events throughout the year and has four canteens or restaurants spread over the south-west. It even runs apprenticeships for budding chefs and award qualifications in restaurant, bar and hotel work. Adding to all this, it decided to start the River Cottage Festival in 2016. The organisers see it as a natural progression from all the other River Cottage events they have been organising over the years.

Lydia Brammer is part of the festival organising team. 'We decided to have a two-day festival in September,' she explains. 'We have a small team that came up with the idea. Last year we did a summer fair but we wanted something with a stronger identity. We always organise a fair every year and we have events throughout the year and there has always been a musical element and so we came up with the idea of music and food together. We have camping here for the first time so we think it now can be classed as a festival.'

Are you already doing something well that could expand into a festival?

Emma Fernandez set up the Purbeck Festival with a group of volunteers. 'The first year I did everything myself but in the second year I had some help,' she says. 'Most important is that it needs people to buy into the idea of a festival. I did a lot of research initially and it ran for two weeks. There are children's events as well. From my perspective, I wanted our festival to work for local people and incomers. I always make sure there is something that works for libraries and schools.'

CHECK OUT THE COMPETITION

Who is doing something similar? For example, Miles Halton runs the Great Dorset Chilli Festival, winning the award for the best chilli festival in 2015. 'I went along to see a chilli festival in Chichester and loved it!' he says. 'It was about the time when I was moving to Dorset from Sussex in 2002 and when we arrived I knew that was something I was going to set up down here because Dorset is a great place for unusual festivals and also there are lots of artisan food producers in the west country. When I started the festival there were four chilli festivals in the country and in 2015 there were about forty-six but we are certainly one of the biggest.'

Think about adapting the theme of an existing festival.

Enthusiasm is vital

This may seem pretty obvious but you must be enthusiastic about your festival. It's no good simply thinking that a festival would be a good idea and what sort should it be, you have to communicate the *excitement* to your helpers and to your audiences. Tanya Bruce-Lockhart, who runs the Bridport Literary Festival says, 'The first thing for anyone who takes on the running of a literary festival is that they must love books and love reading and *enjoy* reading. That enthusiasm has to be passed to an audience. The same applies to any other sort of festival. You must *love* what you are planning to do.'

GROW YOUR FESTIVAL ORGANICALLY

Oundle is a small market town in Northamptonshire with a population of approximately six thousand people. It has a hugely successful music festival which has been running for thirty-two years. This was started in a small way by music masters at Oundle school as an Organ Week and it wasn't long before this developed a serious following with organists coming from great distances. Over the years the festival has grown, encompassing many different musical events, to become Oundle International Festival and, after a few difficult years, is now under the direction of artistic director Kenneth Richardson, formerly director of Covent Garden Festival of Opera and Music.

'It was a difficult situation because the previous festival director retired and the festival bumped along for a while,' he explains. 'The festival is now completely unconnected with the school, although we do use the school premises and we also use other premises. When I arrived I said I wanted to do a couple of things; one was to broaden the appeal of the festival because it was rather classical music-orientated. I do believe that festivals are a reflection of the community in which they exist and they have to offer something to the whole community and not just part of it. The other thing I wanted to do was to create an arts hub around the office that we have which is in the centre of Oundle and is also Oundle box office. We are now offering box office services to other organisations so we sell tickets for our own events and events at Peterborough, Corby and other local places in the area. It's kept busy with people coming in and out all the time.'

MAINTAINING THE ATMOSPHERE

Sometimes a festival can develop in a way that is contrary to the original plans of the organisers and that means its unique features can disappear.

James Shepard started Larmer Tree in 1990. It's now a lot bigger and a lot longer and is quite a different event from when it first began, but it still has the same atmosphere as it had in the first year. That's what James and his team try and maintain. 'In the seventies I went to a festival in South Hill Park near Bracknell, which is an arts centre in a country house set in a beautiful Georgian garden,' says James. 'It is a beautiful setting and it was a jazz festival and I really enjoyed it. From then on I really wanted to do something myself. I was looking for a venue and I didn't just want a farmer's field; I wanted a beautiful space, and Larmer Tree Gardens is just that. My father is a farmer and he said to me, "If you are going to gamble, only gamble as much as you are prepared to lose." That was the attitude I took in the early years. Although it wasn't a very big festival at the beginning, the risk was not minimal.

'If I started it again I don't think I'd change anything. In 1990 it was a different world. I think we all think it was easier when we started out and it's more difficult now but that's because we're older. In those days communication was not easy but it has all changed dramatically since then. Every festival I go to is unique but we are lucky because we have the Larmer Tree Gardens which are pretty special in their own right. The beauty of the whole place is that it's laid out to be a place of entertainment. It's a garden where music is performed. It is run by the Rushmore estate. We take it over for three weeks. And although we run the festival for five days, people can come and camp for that whole week.'

Paul Kelly was involved with that same Bracknell Jazz Festival in the late seventies. 'It was probably the leading jazz festival of its day and I didn't do a huge amount on that, but it was great being around it and seeing how it was done. It involved putting up a very large marquee seating about 1000 to 1500 people. There were two other venues and they pulled in a lot of people locally and from London as it is in driving distance. They put on a lot of international acts.'

> Consider your venue and how easy it is to reach. Festivals can be low on audiences if they are too remote.

WHY FESTIVALS FAIL

You have already read about the experiences of some expert festival organisers and why their festivals are thriving. Not all do. When the Oundle Festival of Literature was launched it ran very successfully for ten years. 'It started with just a few of us putting twenty-five pounds into the pot,' says Paula Prince, one of the organisers, 'and deciding to have a festival for just a weekend. It gradually grew to four days, then a week and then it went to a fortnight.' It was very successful with top authors taking part but a mixture of circumstances was its downfall.

'The festival ran for ten years and in the tenth year everything went wrong,' she explains. 'I had to take over the whole thing. The person booking the authors left, the chairman decided he wanted a year off, the publicity person went, others moved away and it just left me. We only had six months to go until the next festival so what I did was invite authors we had had in the past to come back. And then it stopped. It went on to hold regular all-year-round events and that's what is happening now.'

A very sad scenario involved a festival that was planned for a major city. Organised by a very successful marketing person, a venue was chosen, speakers booked, posters and flyers put around and everything possible was done to promote it. Yet with only a week to go, just a dozen tickets were sold. For some unknown reason, the festival was not supported by the city and worse, by the people who appeared to be so enthusiastic at the beginning. Remember to look at what other events could be happening at the same time. For this particular festival there was nothing so it seemed to be down to the ticket pricing. The prices were high for a first festival – £12.50 per event. This could be a very fair price if a well-known person is speaking but to begin with you should keep the ticket prices as low as you can. You need to entice people to come along because they will not know what to expect and if they can enjoy a first event then it is more likely they will come to more. Be prepared to break even or make a loss on a first festival. It is, after all, a learning curve and ticket prices can rise gradually over the years. If you have done your calculations correctly, taking into consideration all the costs involved in putting on the event, you stand a good chance of breaking even. Whatever you do, don't try to make a profit for the sake of it.

> Keep ticket prices down for your initial events.

Be prepared for hard work

Make no mistake, running a successful festival is tough, both mentally and physically. A festival that runs smoothly does so because of the effort put in by the organiser. This is something that Paul Kelly, organiser of the Bournemouth Jazz Festival, feels strongly.

'First of all, as much as they are enjoyable, festivals are incredibly hard work,' he says. 'Make it very clear about what you want to achieve and how much time you are willing to put in. Make sure there is a clear focus. It's very easy to spread things out over such a range that it loses a sense of focus and coherence and you miss the essence of the festival because it is spread over such a wide range. Look at the nature of the space or spaces you are going to be working in very carefully and think about the programme in relation to it. It's about atmosphere, access, can the audience get there easily? Can the artists get there easily? What are the technical issues?'

A question of time

It is very important to give yourself enough preparation time. You can't decide to start a festival and expect to hold it in a couple of months. Acts and speakers are booked early and don't wait for you to engage them. The same applies to venues. I can't stress enough that a long lead time is necessary to put everything in place and this applies certainly to your first festival.

Diana Bowerman started the Sidmouth Literary Festival and has learnt the value of allowing enough time, remembering that things can go wrong. 'Start early!' she says. 'It takes a lot of time to organise a literary festival. You are chasing people all the time. This year we had an author cancel about a month before the festival and after the programme had come out. I found someone else but then the original author said she could come after all, but we managed to fit in an extra talk.'

QUESTIONS TO ASK YOURSELF BEFORE COMMITTING TO A FESTIVAL

You have made your decision: you *want* to have a festival and it *must work*. Whether you are planning a small village flower festival or a city literary festival, the basic principles are the same. Ask yourself the following questions and if you can answer them positively and confidently, you are on your way:

- Are there people who are enthusiastic and will commit themselves to help? You need volunteers, with different skills, to see the whole project through and not pull out after a few weeks.
- When will you hold the event? Will it clash with other events?
- Where will you hold it? If it's a flower festival it would be in the church so the venue is no problem but what if it is a food festival, a jazz festival or a literary festival?
- How will you fund it? Who can you turn to for money? You will need to spend money before the festival on things such as printing and possibly public liability insurance.

- Can you say, hand on heart, that you are really, *really* committed and honestly prepared to give up many other things in your life to concentrate on the festival?

There is more about this in Chapter Three but if these basic questions are easily and honestly answered then it's time to look into the idea of holding a festival very seriously.

HOW TO IMPROVE

You may be reading this book because you are already running a festival. It's always useful to look critically at the processes in planning and organisation. So, no less than a month after the last event, ask yourself the following questions:

- Are your audiences increasing? Or are they starting to get bored, is there a sense of sameness each year?
- Are you making money? Do you need to review ticket prices?
- Do the venues work or can they be improved? Have you added or changed anything that has improved the enjoyment (such as a pop-up café or a crèche)?
- Is it harder or easier to find new acts, speakers or stallholders? Are people contacting *you* with suggestions rather than you having to contact everyone?
- Are your volunteers as enthusiastic as they were at the beginning? Do they come up with ideas? Do you thank them with a party after the festival is over?
- Are you feeling jaded? Are you getting excited about the next festival and planning it in your head? Or is it becoming a chore?

Think about these six points seriously, especially the last one. This book should help you to formalise your thoughts, give you new and positive ideas and help you through a difficult time.

SUMMARY

- Don't feel daunted. The festivals that have become famous annual events began in a very small way and over the years have improved and grown, through the hard work and inspiration of their organisers
- If you have a burning passion for something you want to turn into a festival, then go for it! That's how many festivals were started
- Use your local assets and connections and any specific local interests to weave into your festival events
- As your festival grows make sure it continues to reflect the interests of the whole community
- It's important to try and maintain the atmosphere of the festival as it grows, so that you don't lose the special characteristics that made it special when it was small
- Not all festivals succeed, so remember that a festival is only as good as the commitment of the organisers
- If you have already run your first festival use this book to help you look critically at the way it was run and consider how the organisation could be improved

2
Putting together a working team

One person, the organiser, has to be in control; that person has taken on the responsibility and will make the final decisions, but they do need a team of people with different skills who are available to help.

CHOOSING YOUR TEAM

If it is a small festival and you have all the necessary skills and feel you can cope, you will not need to assemble a team. I know several organisers who manage alone, apart from taking on extra help just before and during the festival. But you'll need to be very clear about what needs doing to ensure the festival runs smoothly and is a success.If in doubt, however, it is much better to assemble a team of appropriately skilled people around you to help with the considerable task ahead.

You will need to think carefully about who you invite to be part of your team. It's no good choosing people who are enthusiastic but offer no skills. You don't need people who never cook and are not interested in the experience of good food if you are planning a food festival, or people who don't read books (there are quite a few around) helping to organise a literary festival. People who sit round a table and say, 'That's a good idea' or 'That's not a good idea' are useless. In the end you will find there are just a few people doing all the work and everyone else is taking the credit. Recruit people who know their subject and are committed to the festival. Don't be tempted to recruit for enthusiasm alone. Some people would be best used as volunteers or even organisers for the volunteers – as long as they are committed to the festival.

Commitment, and understanding what that entails, is of paramount importance for a successful festival. It is especially important to assess the commitment of those people you decide you want on the team. Some people may be committed at the beginning, when the idea is first suggested, but this commitment may be merely enthusiasm that could wane when they realise the amount of work involved. Be prepared for this.

RECRUITING APPROPRIATE SKILLS FOR THE CORE TEAM

Having decided that you do want to assemble a core team you'll need to find the following people:

- someone with secretarial skills
- someone to take on the role of event manager
- someone with a financial background for the role of treasurer
- someone with public relations (PR) and marketing experience to take responsibility for publicising the event

These four people form a core team and each one can recruit people to help in their specific field. It eases the workload if people are chosen for specific jobs who really have an aptitude and know what they are doing. Jane Corry, from Sidmouth Literary Festival, has strong views about this.

'I think you have to appoint specialist people to deal with all the different jobs that need to be done at a festival,' says Jane. 'For example, you need someone to do PR, somebody to find the authors, somebody who can organise the hospitality, so that one person or a few people are not doing everything. You have to allow these people enough autonomy so that they can do these things without having constantly to refer back. You need somebody in control and ideally somebody who has got the time. We put something in the local paper asking if there was anyone who had spare time and expertise in various areas, particularly marketing and fundraising.'

The role of the secretary

It is worth paying someone to take on secretarial duties if you cannot get a volunteer. To begin with, the work might take up a couple of hours a week that would increase as the festival approaches. Maybe someone with school-age children would fit the bill? The secretary keeps tabs on all decisions made, takes minutes at meetings, writes to performers and keeps files on each, sends out contracts and generally assists the festival organiser and the events manager.

The role of the events manager

Managing events takes time and involves working with different people and organisations. The first thing an event manager has to do is find the venues and book them. He or she has to make sure the venues are suitable, that they have enough chairs and tables, that there is technical equipment – microphones, loudspeakers, and music playback. Is there a caretaker who can move tables and chairs around? The events manager works closely with the organiser and the secretary because the venues must be appropriate.

> You need someone methodical with organisational skills.

The role of the treasurer

The treasurer, to put it simply, looks after the money. He or she should be on hand during the festival to sell tickets and pay artists, authors, speakers, etc. Ask performers to have an invoice for the agreed fee ready to give you at the end of their event and you will save a great deal of time. Everything is then sorted out on the day and saves the trouble of sending out invoices and posting cheques later on.

> An ideal person has bookkeeping or accountancy skills.

The role of PR and marketing

Without good marketing and publicity, people won't know about your festival in the first place. It is absolutely vital to get this aspect right. For this reason Chapter 8 is devoted to these tasks, but for now remember that, when choosing the right team member, it's important to make sure that the person you recruit really understands what the task involves. The main things to bear in mind are:

- you need an excellent communicator to take on this role
- it should be someone who has experience dealing with radio, TV, local newspapers and magazines

As Luke Hasell of Valley Fest puts it, 'Get a great team around you and let them do their thing. We have some brilliant people in the team for Valley Fest and we have all pulled together to create a great festival!'

SHOULD YOU COMMIT TO A COMMITTEE?

It is not always necessary to have a committee. Everyone has to agree on what has to be done and meetings can be time-consuming and not always productive. If you do decide to go down that route, be sure to work out if the members will gel as a team. Individually, they could come across as very pleasant, knowledgeable, enthusiastic and dedicated people but what happens when they are together as a group? Does one person dominate the proceedings? Do some people clearly annoy others? Is there disharmony? Paul Kelly of Bournemouth Jazz Festival sums it up. 'Sometimes you can discover that the team staging the events is rather dysfunctional and there are major personality clashes going on underneath. I think the people side of a festival needs a set of principles and a certain amount of flexibility.'

Before inviting people to join a committee think about bringing them together informally to chat about your ideas. You can tell a lot from such an initial meeting. Afterwards, there will be at least one person who you feel you can trust and with whom you can discuss the meeting.

Make sure you have a strong chairman for your committee.

Do not dismiss the idea of working with a committee. Some are excellent with all the members pulling together, helping each other and enjoying the excitement of the build-up towards the event. For example, former journalist and news editor Diana Bowerman, who started the Sidmouth Literary Festival, is very happy to work with a committee. 'Get together a group of, say, six or eight like-minded people who are prepared to put in the legwork to organise the festival,' she says. 'Hold regular meetings and update everyone by email. At Sidmouth we formed an executive committee and with a treasurer who is an accountant. I am the secretary, and we allocated tasks; we have a sub-committee for hospitality and a publicity committee.'

Make sure everyone is kept informed of the progress.

Another festival that runs with a committee is the Fringe in the Fen at Fenstanton. 'We invited lots of people from the village asking if they would like to be on a committee,' said co-organiser Lynda Symonds. 'We used to meet once a month. I think the thing is not to give anybody too much responsibility and to make it fun. So there is never any back-stabbing or moaning and Nigel and I know the buck stops with us. And we have a really good atmosphere.'

Although Diana and Lynda find it easy to work with a committee and sub-committees, it's worth remembering that committees, depending on who is on them, are not necessarily the best way to prepare for a festival. The majority of people I have spoken to are festival organisers who are in total charge of their festival and take on extra help as necessary. Who was it who said a camel is a horse designed by a committee?

WORKING INDEPENDENTLY

Sometimes, rather than assembling a committee, it might be sensible to have just an organiser who reports to trustees. The role of a trustee is to make sure that the festival is financially viable and to ensure that plans and budgets are feasible. There is generally a board of trustees and they work within two sets of rules: the constitution of the group, and the law. (See Chapter 4). If your festival becomes a charity then you will have to work with trustees.

Several festival organisers prefer to work this way. Tanya Bruce-Lockhart, who started the successful Bridport Literary Festival, reports to trustees. Otherwise she works independently, finding the speakers, liaising with publishers, booking venues, preparing the programme and dealing with publicity. 'During the festival week I have help but otherwise I do the whole thing myself,' she says. For Tanya, this is not difficult, as for many years she was an arts programmes producer for ITV and has many contacts in the media. 'I'm terribly bad at delegating!' she continues. 'I have a bank of stewards for the festival and I have a girl who does a rota for them. We have to sort out various things such as the accommodation if that is necessary and who is going to meet and greet.'

Emma Fernandez started Purbeck Literary Festival in 2014 without any help as part of her PR and marketing work. She had been asked to promote the Isle of Purbeck as a whole and starting a festival became an important part of her strategy. At that time, she said, it was the first literary festival of the season, something she considered important because people who were keen to go to a festival were likely to attend the first one they saw advertised, and choose Purbeck. Venues at Purbeck are varied and include village halls, schools, country pubs, cafés and hotels. This means that festival-goers are not confined to one area and learn something about its history and its facilities. It is a good way to contribute to its economy. Like Tanya, Emma organised the first festival on her own, but finding this took far more time that she expected she recruited some help so that she could concentrate on her other PR work.

TAKE SOME GOOD ADVICE

I believe it is very important to seek out local advice even if you feel you know exactly how you want to run your festival. Tell people what kind of festival you plan. Talk to people, particularly those who can make practical suggestions – such as caterers and food shops for food festivals, musicians for music festivals and bookshop owners for literary festivals. You will be surprised how enthusiastic they can become and how they may offer advice and solutions to possible problems.

Dorchester Literary Festival was started in 2015 by Janet Gleeson and Paul Atterbury, who felt that the county town of Dorset deserved a festival, with its Thomas Hardy and T. E. Lawrence connections. They sensibly took advice before they started organising their festival.

'Very early on, we went and spoke to the town council and Dorchester Arts and they were very much in the loop although we were very keen to remain independent,' says co-director Janet Gleeson. 'We wanted to be linked in but we didn't want to get involved in large, unwieldy committees. Both Paul and I have always worked for ourselves and we like to get on and get things done. It's much easier to say, "Shall we do this?" and then have a discussion and get on with it rather than having interminable meetings about whether you do something or not.'

Paul and Janet sought advice from a variety of people who knew more than they did about festivals. They went to see other festivals and talked to the organisers, finding everyone very helpful. As Janet says, 'You must talk to people who have run or are running similar festivals and get advice from them. You need to get a good idea about what to expect.'

LET THE FESTIVAL GROW NATURALLY

Remember that nothing stays the same; your festival will either grow or decline. It should grow but not too quickly. Each year the festival will be different. You will find that if you have addressed problems that occurred in the previous year they should not occur again – but others might. Once an audience has enjoyed a festival they talk about it and the following year more tickets are sold. Revenue will increase and you can expand.

As a festival grows in size so the demands on the festival organiser and the team become greater and often more complicated. For instance, the venues you use may be too small to accommodate more people. You could have a problem here in finding a larger venue. You will find that speakers, performers and artists begin to approach *you* and ask to be part of the festival. When this happens it is time to have a serious talk with your team.

- Do you want to add another day?
- Can you add an extra event on the days you already have?

Know your audience

Take a serious look at the people who make up your audience. This is where a questionnaire is useful (see Chapter 11). Are they mainly retired? Young families? Professionals? Artistic? Music lovers? You need to put on events that interest them.

> Give the people what they want.

You may have to get more people involved but the secret lies in how you deploy them. Kenneth Richardson explains how he organises the growing Oundle International Festival. 'We have a huge army of volunteers and a very small number of salaried staff,' he says. 'The volunteers get to see shows and we usually have a get-together in the run-up to the festival which is a briefing and a festival launch.' The festival developed naturally without putting too much extra strain on the organising team.

SUMMARY

- Take care in selecting the right sort of team to work with you
- Define the roles of key members of the festival team
- Talk to local organisations, such as the town council and prominent local people about feasibility
- Do not rush things. Allow the festival to develop naturally

3

Researching and developing your idea

Once you have the embryo of a festival there are several very important decisions you have to make at the beginning of the process.

It is worth thinking through the following points carefully. The more planning and research that you can do beforehand the better. You will be prepared and confident and secure in the knowledge that you have done everything you can do. Make copious notes so that you can refer to them when necessary.

Considering joining the Association of Festival Organisers (AFO – www.festivalorganisers.org). This organisation shares information and supports members to improve the festival scene. The general secretary is Steve Heap who has been involved in festivals for more than forty-five years. The AFO holds regular conferences and training sessions and membership offers many useful benefits.

Make sure you are covered with public liability insurance. People are often litigious and you don't want to be sued if someone trips and sprains an ankle. Research health and safety. Much of the information you need is available in *The*

Purple Guide to Health, Safety and Welfare at Music and Other Events. This both covers legislation and gives event organisers information about best practice and issues that need to be considered when events are being organised. It is available online and for a small subscription is a valuable source of information (www.purpleguide.co.uk).

CHOOSING PERFORMERS, SPEAKERS AND ACTS

If you are planning a music festival, it is of course important to make sure you go and listen to live music. But don't leave it at that. Talk to other people in the audience while you're there. Ask what they thought of the acts – if one band was better or worse than they expected. Get into a conversation. The same goes for speakers. You must hear them! If you are planning a food festival see how inspiring the demonstrators are.

Lydia Brammer agrees. 'Do your research,' she says. 'We learnt to go and see and hear as many bands as we could. You really do need to see and hear them in the flesh and performing live. It's important not to just rely on music videos because they are all put together nicely and everybody comes across as amazing. You have to see them live or watch a lot of live YouTube videos. And you have to do that early on in your planning so you get a choice. Weather has a big impact and if it gets muddy in the fields then there will be problems with parking. We have to make sure we have lots of undercover spaces so if it does rain there are places for people to go and hide.'

Always listen to bands and speakers before you book them.

CONSIDER YOUR COMMITMENT

Do you honestly have the time to run a festival? It takes up a lot of time and it's a lot of hard work so the person taking on the festival must be prepared for this. If you have a full-time job, if you have demanding children or if you do something else that takes much of your time and energy, organising a festival is not for you. Think carefully because it is not something you can start and then leave after a few months. There will rarely be a break because so often a problem crops up or a new decision that has to be made at short notice and you have to be able to sort it out.

Running a festival is hard work – and is *continuously* hard work.

Ensuring your commitment is something that Kenneth Richardson strongly advises. 'If you want to start a festival you have to be completely dedicated,' he says. 'You have to be slightly mad and you have to believe absolutely in what you are doing. If you don't believe in what you are doing, it won't work. It might not work even if you *do* believe in what you are doing but you've got to have faith in it. If you don't actually have faith in it there's no point in even starting. And do be prepared for the unexpected. No matter how well you plan, something will come up. It *always* happens!'

31

DON'T DUPLICATE

Find out where the nearest festivals are and when they are held. Look within a twenty-mile radius. Be careful if there is something similar and even if there is another event of any kind. It doesn't matter if they are quite different – music, science, wood-whittling – they could considerably deplete your audience. Other nearby festivals held at a different time of the year from the one you are planning may take your star attractions and your potential audience especially if they are established and you are not. People become festival-fatigued.

You want to hold your festival when there is little competition and then it's a good idea to keep it at the same time each year. Holding your festival at different times each year confuses people.

I believe that each festival is unique and if you plan sensibly there should not be a problem. In my case, a similar festival started five miles away. Everyone was worried. It was in a larger town with a permanent theatre which was a huge advantage. But there was one difference and that was in the audience. We had an audience who wanted to learn, but theirs was a crowd who wanted to be entertained. I went to hear a friend talking about his new book. He was scheduled to come to our festival three weeks later and I wanted to see the size and make-up of his audience. It consisted of fewer than twenty people and at the time we had already sold more than seventy tickets.

> If there are similar festivals happening around the time of yours or even at another time of the year make sure your festival stands out.

TIMES AND DATES

Will your big date fall over a weekend and how long will you run for – three days . . . or even five? For your first festival it is sensible to keep the running time fairly short and I would recommend a weekend or maybe three days as maximum. You are bound to find that problems occur that you have never considered and you will realise what improvements you can make.

Do not try to be ambitious. If you are not within walking distance of a railway station or a bus stop, you must be aware of possible parking problems. Many people will come by car. Keep that first festival short and simple because I can't emphasis enough how exhausting it can be.

There are so many times when it is not sensible to hold a festival: during the school term, for instance, is not a great time to run children's events unless you can run them on a Saturday or a Sunday. But then the school holidays present their own problem – many families will take a break but older people seem to steer clear of these times; it much depends on the type of festival you are holding. In September older people often seem to go off on a cruise (because prices are lower than they are in school holidays and there are no children around!) and the dark, cold nights of January and February do not encourage people to leave their firesides. In a way, you just have to pick the time that is most suitable and convenient for everyone in your team and keep your fingers crossed.

Sometimes circumstances out of your control will force you to run your festival to fit in with other events. 'We were spawned by the Bridport Prize which was started thirty-five to forty years ago as a source of income for Bridport Arts

Centre,' explains Tanya Bruce-Lockhart. 'It was for short-story writing and poetry. The winners are always announced in November. Despite misgivings about having a festival in November we felt we had to fit in and since then we have always held the Bridport Festival at that time.'

DO NOT RUSH INTO PRODUCTION

The committee at Sidmouth believe they could have done with a few more weeks to plan. They chose a weekend in June to involve visitors to the seaside town. 'With the first festival we tried to do children's events at the main venue but it didn't work,' says secretary Diana Bowerman. 'June is a difficult month for children because the older ones are doing exams. We invited the author Jane Corry to be our writer-in-residence and it ended up with Jane and I, with a few other helpers, planning all the events. There came a point when we wondered if it was worth carrying on because there was such a lot to do and we only had two months but I felt that Jane had been so proactive, giving up her writing time to get involved with the festival, it would have been unfair to her if we stopped. It would also put her in an awkward position with the authors she had invited. So we carried on.'

Be flexible about altering your plans.

Elizabeth Turnbull, organiser of the Leigh Food Festival, checks for anything that might impact on numbers. 'First of all, make sure you've got a date that doesn't clash with anything else happening in the area that could take away your audience. I don't want Leigh Food Festival to clash with events in the next village or with the Wimbledon weeks.'

The weather

Glastonbury festival-goers seem to love wallowing in lots of mud – the more the better! Just don't count on that spirit for your own festival. 'We are quite dependent on the weather,' says Miles Halton of the Great Dorset Chilli Festival. 'It makes a huge amount of difference. One year we had torrential rain first thing on the Saturday morning and the numbers were down to about sixty per cent of what they should have been. It cleared up after about an hour and a half but people had made alternative plans. It does have a massive effect.'

The Great Dorset Chilli Festival takes place over a summer weekend. It was started in 2011 in the National Trust house of Kingston Lacy before moving to St Giles, another grand house, in Wimborne, in 2012. 'The house is surrounded by three hundred acres,' says Miles, 'and it's a stunning location. The parkland has open fields and there are three main areas for the festival so there is not everything in one big circle. A lot of the traders come with their own gazebos and it is very colourful. I had to make sure there was enough interest to warrant spending a day at the festival if a family come along and only one person loves chilli! There has to be a reason for bringing the children otherwise you are excluding too many people.'

Lynda Symonds of the Fringe in the Fen Festival planned a summer festival. 'We decided to hold the Fringe in the Fen Festival in July before the school holidays started and we were hoping that the weather would be kind. In 2016 it coincided nicely with the anniversary of the birth of Lancelot "Capability" Brown.'

Another July festival is the Larmer Tree Festival. 'We decided to hold it in July because I overheard someone in the pub saying that the second weekend in July had the best chance of good weather and I believed them!' says organiser James Shepard.

> Long-term weather forecasts can help you plan – use with caution!

English weather is famously unpredictable (although someone once told me that 17 May was always dry). Even given the most advanced forecasting technology, the unconvinced go out with both sunglasses and an umbrella. But, if you are clever, the weather need not be a problem. The layout of the three food marquees at the Sturminster Newton Cheese Festival in mid-September means that visitors can go from one marquee to another without getting soaking wet in a rainstorm.

Several literary festivals chose the end of the year to have a festival. 'We decided to hold our literary festival in November largely because of our own schedules,' says Janet Gleeson of Dorchester Festival. 'Paul goes to Australia in the New Year for three months on lecture tours and then he goes walking in May and then it's the *Antiques Roadshow* (in which we are both involved) to consider so the autumn was the obvious time. From the point of view of books, that is the time most people buy books.'

Choose the best days of the week

Should you go for midweek or over the weekend? This is something that Jane Corry learnt after the first Sidmouth

Festival. She says it's important to take school terms into consideration. 'One thing we learnt from our first year was that the children's events we held at the festival on Saturday didn't attract that many children because they were all doing sporty things. The following year we sent authors into the schools, where they were welcomed. It meant children were able to meet the authors and not miss out.

'We are changing our festival from Friday and Saturday to Saturday and Sunday. Although there are a lot of retired people in Sidmouth, there are also a lot of people who work. When we held our How to Get Published day, which was hugely successful, we did have people say it was a shame it was on a Friday because they couldn't make it. A weekend is a good time to have a festival and two days is long enough. Some festivals go on for quite a long time and that is very wearing on the organisers. I think two days is enough or three days, maximum. One day is never quite enough. It's a question of knowing your market and what people do in your town.'

AN EXTRA DIMENSION

Do try and make your festival not only different from others but unique to your part of the world. For example, if you have decided to hold a food festival because there is a world-famous chef working at a local hotel or a cider festival because you are bang in the area where cider apples grow, see what you can do to encourage the widest audience. Run a competition well ahead of the event with a prize presented to the winners at the event. If you charge an entry fee that could help defray costs.

SUITABLE VENUES

You may want several halls to accommodate different sizes of audience or a theatre. There may be a field on which you can erect marquees (providing you intend to hold your festival between May and September). If you hire a marquee, then you must also include portable toilets. Check what the costs are likely to be. You must be able to accommodate audiences of different sizes if you are running a literary or music festival – for example, for twenty-five-plus, fifty-plus and three hundred-plus. It is not easy to gauge how many people a speaker or a band will attract but, obviously, the better known they are, the more popular they will be. You will find that you are having to spend more than you are budgeting for but try and work out the basic costs well before the festival begins. (See Chapter 4 on finance).

Sponsorship and complimentary tickets

Always negotiate your costs. Many people are only too pleased to help a new enterprise and I am a great believer in giving out free tickets as a thank-you. Apart from anything else, free-bies are a handy way of getting the numbers up at an event. If you have already sold out, you could suggest your sponsor meets the performers for a post-event drink or meal.

Crowd size matters

Some speakers or demonstrators stipulate the size of audience they need to make their appearance worthwhile. If you find yourself in the position in which relatively few tickets have been sold for someone you expected to be a great draw, be proactive and move the event to a smaller venue. There is nothing worse than having half a dozen people listening to someone speaking in a hall that accommodates five hundred. It is dispiriting for the speaker and could be fatal for your reputation. One author I know was invited to speak in a large theatre. The organisers confidently told the author's publisher that there would be at least forty people in attendance. After a three-hour journey, the author discovered there were sixteen in the audience – including some of the theatre staff. Neither he nor his publisher was impressed. Needless to say, that gaffe meant that next time those festival organisers requested an author from that publisher they weren't given the warmest of welcomes. Another example: I went to hear a high-profile author friend talking at a local literary festival. It was in the library and twenty chairs had been set out. But there just were nine in the audience and five of those were library staff. A bookseller was on hand to sell my friend's work but had only brought a handful of her latest hardback and none of her back catalogue. Nevertheless, her talk was excellent – but you can be sure that her feedback to her publishers was damning.

Hopefully, with all the advice you've been reading here, you will find your event goes very well – perhaps your speaker proves very informative and gives such a memorable show that you want them back the following year. Word will get around and their next visit will encourage a bigger audience and that's how you can begin to expand.

As the festival develops, you will learn lessons about the size of the venue you need and the size of the stage. Learn about the needs of the different events (the big band, the high-profile author) so that you can satisfy them. Using only one venue to host all events was practical in Sidmouth. They have one large building with rooms of different sizes and having everything in close proximity made the events easier to organise.

'It helped that we could hold the festival in one big building,' explains Jane Corry. 'It worked very well and we had one room as a green room. I think we had a high level of hospitality because everybody made dishes and there was a constant supply of food.'

- Remember, speakers compare their experiences with each other on the festival circuit and the last thing you need is a black mark against your festival.
- If you are running a literary or book festival, check that the bookseller has ordered back catalogue stock and also some paperbacks. It gets expensive for festival-goers if they have to buy a ticket and only have the option of a pricey hardback.

KNOW YOUR TARGET AUDIENCE

Do you expect to see those who are well-off, middle-class and prepared to support a festival? Are they retired and likely to enjoy and support a festival on their doorstep? Are they young families with enough spare energy to get involved? Or, at best, are they a mixture of all these? If the answer is 'Yes' to any of these questions, congratulations – you know how to tailor your festival.

One literary festival with which I was involved could not get decent audiences for young women writers of commercial fiction. They arranged events for mornings, afternoons, evenings and on Saturdays and Sundays, but they did not bring in decent numbers. The local bookseller said the authors' books sold very well, they were well known, their events were well publicised and yet few people came to hear them speak about their books. Could it be because this style of writing is also often known as 'chick-lit'? For me, the term is a derogatory way of referring to a genre whose authors write very well and whose feel-good books leave the reader happy and satisfied, but it is perhaps one that people just don't take as seriously as they should.

As Tanya Bruce-Lockhart of Bridport Literary Festival says, 'Putting together a programme of events to appeal to all as well as those with specific interests is very much a case of "knowing your audience". I am very mindful that the people who are available to come to events during the day are the retired or who can make some time available during a working day to attend and I programme accordingly. In the evenings I try to do events where there is a younger audience and people who work full-time. Having worked in arts programmes for ITV, I have the advantage of being able to find my way around the publishing business and have good contacts with writers, publishers and their ancillary departments.'

Aim to give the audience what they want and not what you think they *ought* to see.

Paula Prince, of the Oundle Festival of Literature, says that you have to balance a sense of being in touch with your audience with the need to be methodical and organised, which is 'not the easiest thing when there is so much going on around you. You really have to do your research. If you are prepared you will be all right.' Consult widely to make sure you have considered everyone who might be interested. 'Remember to talk to the book groups. And you have to get your publicity right,' she says. 'If you've got a gardener coming along, you make sure all your gardening clubs in the area know about it. You have to be quite eclectic with who you have but the main thing is to have fun!'

TICKET TO RIDE

It is crucial to set up a workable, simple way of selling tickets. How will they be sold – online or through shops? If online, will the webmaster be responsible or will punters be able to get them from a variety of outlets? The answers to all these questions will very much depend on the size of the festival. A small village festival with straightforward pricing can be focused on a local shop. You will be involving the shop in the festival and they will spread the word as well as sell the tickets. There will be no need to make your life any more complicated.

If, however, you are planning a larger festival lasting several days, you need to have a professional ticket-selling service in place. For my own first festival, we were encouraged to find local people offering to sell tickets for us and, as we were literature-based, at the time it seemed sensible to have an independent bookshop do it. But that proved to be a mistake. Ticket-selling is, no matter how much you love your own festival yourself, just another chore for the staff in a busy bookshop. In our case, things really did become confused and the result was we never had an accurate account of how many tickets were sold for each event. Hands up – it was totally our fault. We had fifteen events over three days and on top of that we offered a ten per cent discount on tickets sold to members of our own literary society. It was just not fair to expect the bookshop staff to cope with so much extra work.

> Don't burden well-meaning but busy people with the extra responsibility of selling tickets.

We also made an arrangement with the local tourist information centre and this worked much better. They took a percentage of sales but coped with selling tickets at different prices, including those discounts for literary society members. There were still many confusing variables though. Some people also telephoned for tickets and asked if they could pick them up at the door, while others wanted them posted out. And then there was that time we had *two* authors cancel at the last minute; we had to arrange refunds to everyone but in many cases we had no idea how to reach the purchasers. These unforeseen happenings can become a bit of a nightmare on top of everything else you have to do.

It's important to learn from your difficulties. In our case, the following year we decided that we would take a flat rate of one pound off all ticket prices for literary society members instead of ten per cent and that made selling much easier. We also made sure that all buyers gave us their contact details (via a form in the programme) so that we could refund money in the event of cancellation.

- Take care when deciding the best way to sell tickets
- Make buying tickets easy and uncomplicated

The price has to be right

Establishing the cost of a ticket is important but is, at the beginning, really a matter of trial and error. Go too low and you may not cover your costs; too high and people will not come. As author Kate Furnivall said to one festival organiser, 'To be honest, I did wonder, when I saw the high price of the tickets, whether people would be willing to cough up that amount of money and I rather thought that sales might be hit by this. I actually have a group of six friends who were planning on coming but changed their minds when they heard the price of tickets – plus the return train fare. A costly outing.'

Cost out the event by what you need to cover. For example, if you have a technician who does the sound system for the whole festival, break down his fee so that you know how much he or she costs per event. Similarly, any other expenditure such as the cost of the room or hall or marquee should be broken down – you need only do it roughly. I firmly believe that it is best to err on the side of caution. Say that you will spend £250 to put on an event for eighty-five people. That would mean that if every seat were sold, each would have to cost about three pounds for you to break even. If only forty people bought tickets then you would lose quite a lot of money – be sure to build in the possible loss and the going rate for tickets. If the performer is well known you can always factor in a premium but you may have to give a larger fee.

It is better to have a standard amount for all tickets for most events, with higher prices reserved for high-profile appearances. Children's events should always be cheaper or free.

For your first festival, when nobody knows what to expect, charge a fairly low amount for a ticket – £5.00, £7.50 or £8.50.

If you add a glass of wine you could probably say £10 but no more. I know of one festival that was cancelled despite a huge amount of clever publicity because so few people bought tickets.

- Be satisfied with making a small profit for your first festival. You will have attracted an audience who enjoyed the event and they will spread the word so that next year you could have more people who pay an extra pound for a seat.
- If you run over Saturday and Sunday, try offering a weekend ticket that encourages people to go to events they may not have considered.

> Number tickets for seated events to stop people queuing very early and everyone becoming very disgruntled if it rains.

Count your tickets

In our case, our tourist information centre would send us weekly accounts of how many tickets were sold – very professional. A glance at the spreadsheet told us the cost of a ticket per event by members and non-members, total sales, the total amount of money received and how many complimentary tickets were given out. The final column showed the total revenue and the commission taken by the centre. We immediately knew when we had to do more publicity for speakers who were not doing as well as we expected.

As the festival grew, we sold directly from the website as well. These days, more people are keen to buy online as it saves so much time. Remember that there are many older people who do not have computers and prefer to buy tickets over the counter. That said, every festival should have a website. This is where most of your potential audience look for information. Once we had our website up and running it made a significant difference to our ticket sales and many people chose to buy tickets that way. A properly designed website can be expensive but it will pay for itself very quickly and is a valuable addition.

Get online

Try to have a basic website set up as soon as you can and then, when you've made a bit of money, have it profession-ally designed. You'll be surprised what a difference that makes. It will make the festival organiser and the team look more professional and it is not difficult to set up a system to sell tickets. When we first did it we were unsure how many would take advantage of such a facility, but it worked very well. There are some very talented web designers around but do your research and don't be tempted by cheap offers just to save money. Look at other websites and see which you find appealing and then find out who designed them.

TOP OF THE LIST

The first thing on your to-do list should be to make lists. Some people automatically write them, but when you are organis-ing what is likely to be a complicated programme with many aspects, lists are crucial. Everyone who is directly involved should have a copy and ideally, most should be drawn up by the organiser with input from the events manager.

Tanya Bruce-Lockhart makes sure she has covered all eventualities for Bridport Literary Festival. 'The logistics are most important – even more important than getting the programme together,' she says. 'Only one person can do it. You have to make sure that *every* aspect of *each* event is covered. There has to be a list of who is involved, who is meeting and greeting, who is dealing with hospitality, what equipment is needed and who is dealing with that. And then you have to make sure these people have the information and understand the timings. You also need to have at your fingertips what else is needed and any special requirements.'

Helpers and volunteers

You certainly need a list of helpers. These are likely to be volunteers and you must never, *ever* take them for granted. Their committed help is vital, so cosset them and make them feel special and needed – which, of course, they are. Have an informal meeting, perhaps a party with wine and nibbles, well before the festival and let your volunteers in on the plans you have made and tell them who you have invited. Enthuse them with your ideas and excite them with the thought of the festival. They are important people who will help everything run smoothly and you need to get this across to them.

You should also be realistic in your appreciation. Paul Kelly is dismissive about the lack of commitment of some people. 'What you don't need are wishy-washy helpers who suddenly announce, a few days before the start, that they will be going away,' he says. '"Didn't we tell you?" they say. Of course, by whatever universal law that governs these things, these will always be people you have put in important roles and you have quite enough to do without having to try to find replacements at very short notice. Instil in your helpers the importance of their roles and that if there is any possibility, *any possibility at all*, of them not being available from the start of the festival, they *must* tell you as soon as possible.'

After the festival, hold a thank-you evening for the helpers when you can point out how good it has been having such committed volunteers and that you do hope they will be available to help next year. By then you should have the dates of the following year's festival. Make sure these are put in diaries.

CONTINGENCY PLANNING

I believe that, however well you plan, there is always something that comes up that you haven't thought through. Not everyone agrees with me. 'Everyone who is involved with the Fringe in the Fen Festival agrees that our planning is second to none,' says Lynda Ferrier, proudly. 'We plan very, very carefully right down to the dotting of the i's and the crossing of the t's. It's six months' full-time work. You can't do anything else because it's twenty-four-seven. We sell all the tickets and we do online booking. I have to be absolutely sure I am willing to put my life on hold for six months, and that is the first decision we make.'

CLEAR AIMS

Sometimes there is so much to plan that the route to the festival becomes confused. Take the advice Paul Kelly offers: 'Ask yourself what you are trying to achieve,' he says. 'You have to be clear on this because if not, you are going to have a lovely time but the end result will be a bit of a mish-mash. Do you have enough resources – and that can be people – to achieve what you want? Get the money side right. Make sure you have got all your costings done properly and make sure the money side looks sensible on paper. When I ran a jazz festival I built in huge amounts of financial contingency. I made sure that the projected amount we were going to spend was considerably less than we were bringing in, in terms of the grants and the sponsorship and things like that. Everywhere where you are, there is local talent and they want to perform. We set a threshold of trying to pay everybody seventy-five pounds per musician. I had to reduce that a little bit on some events where there was no revenue coming in. But musicians like to perform.'

In a similar way Luke Hasell had a very clear view of what he wanted to achieve at Valley Fest. 'I suppose that we wanted it to have a line-up that could keep you dancing all weekend but not with huge bands that makes it all about the music and command a huge ticket value,' he says. 'We wanted it to celebrate the land, of course, so the main stage overlooks the lake – the most incredible view in the country, I'd argue. And we wanted the food to be wholesome, fresh and delicious. We also love a party so there needed to be plenty of dancing in the tepee valley.'

SUMMARY

- Be clear about the amount of work involved in running a festival
- Make sure you listen to live bands and speakers before booking them

4

Funding your festival

You will need money before the festival begins – much more than you imagine at this stage.

LIST YOUR EXPENSES

If you are starting your first festival, the idea of finding the money to pay for everything can be quite worrying. It need not be if you go about it in a methodical manner.

When we started our literary festival we approached the local council, who gave us a very welcome three thousand pounds. This came from a trust fund established to help new initiatives. We formed a literary society and charged ten pounds annual membership. Members got ten per cent off all books bought at independent bookshops and another ten per cent off tickets. We sent regular newsletters and gave members early booking opportunities. The first year we had three hundred members, bringing in another three thousand pounds.

- Be realistic about listing all expenses. It's easy to underestimate – costs can easily rise without you realising.
- You will find it very worthwhile to research sources of grants and bursaries – there are many organisations that

can help. Your local librarian will usually point you in the right direction.

- Don't forget the council. They are often keen to support local initiatives, especially if they bring tourists into the area and boost the economy.
- Look at local and national charities who will allocate money for good causes.
- Many local businesses are keen to support enterprise.
- The National Lottery is another source if you're not put off by filling in many, many forms. (This is where finding the strengths of your teams is important. Some people actually enjoy doing applications.)

FINDING SPONSORS

Sponsorship is important but you will find it a slog before you have managed to establish yourself. It gets easier after the first festival – everyone likes to have their name connected with successful events. This may take a couple of years so, until then, you'll need all your powers of persuasion and a bulging book of personal contacts along with as much proof as you can find to support your claim that the festival will be a success. Work towards identifying a major sponsor who gives you enough money to cover the big pre-festival outgoings. Never forget, once you've got them, that it would be hard to operate without the help of a sponsor and make sure you show how grateful you are by offering them privileges.

Making sponsorship attractive

Decide how you want to organise sponsorship. You could start with 'supporters of the festival' for a minimum donation. It's surprising how small amounts add up. Small businesses might want to sponsor just one event and a corporation would be more likely to be a main sponsor. Give the big players more privileges than the others. Put their company name on all promotional material. It should definitely be prominent in the programme, where you can offer them a full-page advert and, if you have a banner across a road, for example, include their logo. If there is room, splash that name on the tickets, posters and flyers and, of course, on the website. Offer to put sponsor banners in the main venue and display their promotional material at all events.

Your sponsors are proud to sponsor you. Make sure you give them plenty of publicity.

All sponsors should be offered complimentary tickets; the main sponsor gets comps across the board and individual sponsors tickets for their event. Don't be stingy, especially in your first festival, as the main sponsor might like to bring clients. Sponsors should be given the opportunity to meet the main people involved. It is a good idea to hold a reception for all the sponsors and advertisers before the festival. Choose somewhere attractive and, of course, try to find a sponsor for this event too! Serve wine and nibbles and take the opportunity to thank publicly and by name all the people and businesses sponsoring the festival.

Bring all the sponsors together for a public thank-you. People are often more confident when they see who else is sponsoring an event.

It is very important to display prominently the names of the sponsors. Some festivals do this on a big scale. They grade their personal sponsors by the amount they are prepared to give so they have different levels of sponsorship – platinum, gold, silver, and bronze. I think this is clever because there will be certain people who would never want their name associated with a bronze sponsorship and so will give more money than they first intended.

Pay to play or not to pay to play

There is always the question of whether you charge people who have stalls at the festival. River Cottage's Lydia Brammer is firm about this. 'If it's a static market stall and they are selling their products then we charge for that but if they are *offering* something then we don't usually charge. There is a small market area which is not as big as the food fair and there are people coming along offering different activities and demonstrations and we don't charge them. There is a horse and a falconry show and workshops and we don't charge for those either. Our budget isn't huge and because we are including bands we have had to manage it very carefully.'

Individuals sponsor too

Tanya Bruce-Lockhart has a money-raising system that works for her. 'We don't get any public funding at all,' she says. 'With Bridport not having any commerce or industry, it's been quite difficult to go to organisations in the town because there are so few and those that are there don't have that sort of money. In the end, we decided to approach individuals who had family charitable trusts and people who wanted to become involved with the festival.'

With the Bridport Literary Festival taking place in early November, Tanya produces a schedule of events in May which she circulates to all those who have sponsored in the past. There are layers of funding: £1000 is 'platinum', £500 'gold', £250 'silver' and £125 'bronze'. Tanya asks for £500 to sponsor an event outright, with a shared event at £250. Sponsors get special privileges depending on their level. 'I raise the money,' says Tanya, 'and I hand it over to the chairman of the trustees and the number crunchers.'

Other routes: some festivals have 'friends' who support them. In practice, this is similar to individual sponsorship. Friends donate to the festival and in return receive benefits such as advance copies of the programme, priority booking for events, invitations to regular events and gatherings, invites to an annual party and the opportunity to be involved in various ways with the festival.

Lynda Ferrier says, 'We have sponsorship and sponsors come by word of mouth and local contacts in the village. We have had a private donation towards the festival of a thousand pounds. Sponsorship comes from a variety of sources – from an estate agency, property developers and the local pub to a cattery and kennels.'

Having 'Friends' of your festival reaches those who may want to support the event without doing anything more than donating

Not everyone agrees that sponsorship has benefits. James Shepard already had enough money to risk on the first Larmer Tree Festival and says that it has remained 'a sponsor-free festival because we always wanted to plough our own furrow and there is no such thing as a free meal. As soon as sponsors are involved they want something. The first few festivals did run at a loss. It's like any business when you are starting out although I never saw it as a business. But people started to talk about it and tell their friends and gradually we started to get a following.'

MONEY-MAKING IDEAS

Competitions

There are many ways to raise money. Competitions connected with the festival are very direct. By charging a fee to enter the competition you should be able to cover any costs and you'll keep the festival in the forefront of people's minds. The obvious competitions are written ones – you could ask for poems or short stories connected with the festival – and you could try something that involves local shops. Perhaps stick questions in shop windows. The local newspaper might join in.

Taster events

Let's look at some ideas to inspire you and perhaps raise with your team to encourage them to come up with some of their own.

If you are running a literary festival, invite an author to come and speak and see how big an audience you get (it'll give you an idea of how well you might do in the actual festival). You will pay the author but the fee should easily be covered by ticket sales. Similarly, a music festival could lead in with a night with one band or classical group and, again, you can gauge the local interest at an early stage. A beer festival could have a tasting day, a literary event might have a poetry slam in your local pub.

Kettlewell Scarecrow Festival organises a trail around the village which includes riddles to solve with a daily prize. They charge a pound for a sheet of instructions and the route takes you past the village hall (where you can pop in for a taste of 'real country baking'), the local cafés and the three pubs. They charge a small fee for parking and all the profits go to the church, school, village hall and local projects so it benefits the whole community. The festival itself lasts for nine days in August.

Sidmouth Literary Festival has pre-festival fundraising events. 'One was with Ken Livingstone which was a sell-out,' recalls Diana Bowerman. 'We charged twenty pounds and that was for lunch, a glass of bubbly on arrival and the talk.' Jane Corry adds that they have held raffles as well but advises having a raffle committee to help source the prizes.

Whatever you decide to do, don't forget that if it involves people you should be covered by public liability insurance. This is not particularly expensive and there are many insurance companies that can advise.

GET NETWORKING – AND THEN NETWORK SOME MORE

Once more I have to underline that it is so important to get the word around that there is going to be a festival. You must generate *excitement* and this will come naturally through your own enthusiasm. Diana Bowerman, as a former journalist, knows the value of spreading the word. 'It is really important to do a lot of networking,' she says. 'We had fantastic support from the town and we had several grants for different events. I wrote a general letter inviting clubs and associations to be involved with the festival and that produced a great response. At the festival we had flyers saying, "Would you like to be a friend or a patron?" This was a way of beginning to raise money for next year and getting support.'

Jane Corry agrees. 'I think you should network and *network*,' she says. 'Go to as many festivals as possible and ask the organisers if they would mind giving the details of those who interest you.'

The Dorchester Festival organisers target businesses in the town. 'We started to raise money by going to businesses and telling them what we wanted to do,' says Janet Gleeson, 'and, almost without exception, they were really keen to get involved, which is probably because there was nothing like it in the town. We approached estate agents, solicitors and even builders – and one builder became our main sponsor in the first year.'

Start talking about a festival and people will become intrigued.

MASTER FINANCIAL DETAIL

Pay for important skills

You will need some secretarial help and while there are people who will happily give their time, others could be persuaded by offering a few hours each week for a fee. They will need stationery and will have to develop a good filing system.

What about a treasurer?

This is a fairly straightforward but vital job that can easily be carried out by someone with bookkeeping experience – although at some stage you will need an accountant to audit the books.

Costing the venues

Will you have more than one venue? Do you hire them for the day or just for the event? If your festival takes place over a week or a weekend, can you get a discount? Does the cost include a technician? Will they deal with microphones, laptops, memory sticks, etc.? You'll probably need a caretaker to open up, deal with heating, move chairs around and generally ensure tidiness and cleanliness.

The stars of the show

Authors, performers or speakers are very important to your future festivals, so look after them. Many do the full circuit and they *talk*, to each other and to their agents and publicists. They even talk to other festival organisers. You'll soon hear all about the festivals that let their speakers find their own way to the venues; who look after their stars until they have spoken and then abandon them; and those festivals who never even offer so much as a cup of coffee to their guests.

I cannot stress enough that the people taking part in your festival – be they speakers, musicians, or stallholders – are your greatest asset. The audience is coming to see them and future festivals depend on how the audience react. There's no getting around it – they will cost you money. They will require a fee, they may need accommodation and they may need lunch or supper. Build *all* this into your costings.

At the same time, you don't need to accept the first figure you're given. Try to persuade hotels, restaurants and B&Bs to give you discounts. Convince them that it's good for their business too – if audience members are travelling a distance to hear a speaker in the evening, they may be persuaded to stay overnight if they feel they are getting that special festival-only rate. Remember, you can repay these establishments by giving free or discounted publicity in the festival programme and complimentary tickets to certain events. You need to create as much interest as possible in the forthcoming festival. Think of your local restaurants and coffee shops. Could you ask them to do a special deal for festival-goers?

START SPREADING THE NEWS

Once you have decided you are definitely going to hold your festival, you must begin to ensure the idea is lodged firmly in the minds of local people. By local, I mean the general vicinity where you expect to find your audience.

If yours is a literary festival then, unless there is one already, why not start a literary society? There may be several book clubs but a formal literary group is different. Books are my passion and, having worked for many years in the publishing industry, I am always keen to encourage people to read. In my case, we formed a small committee of five to set up our society and that helped to feed in to the festival. We held a members' evening on 23 April, the anniversary of both Shakespeare's birth and death, and World Book Day. We used the occasion to explain what we hoped to achieve and gave out free books. People were interested and wanted to know more and to become involved.

We then held a literary lunch with an author as speaker and this attracted still more people. Attendees were starting to ask us what was planned for the next event. We decided to invite an author to talk about her books and her writing and so we held an evening with Joanne Harris, whose books famously include *Chocolat*. We were offered the use of a large marquee and served bellinis, those exotic peach-based cocktails, in deference to Joanne's then new book, *Peaches for Monsieur le Curé*. This was in July when we expected to have a lovely, warm summer evening. But no! It had started raining a couple of days earlier and that evening it simply bucketed down. Would people brave the weather? We were doubtful but, yes, they did. Over two hundred struggled through driving rain and flooded streets and dripped into the marquee. That event, despite the weather, also helped funding for the festival.

Whatever type of festival you are planning, it is easy to adapt these ideas. Instead of a literary society, start a group that reflects your festival such as a music group or if there is already such a group, then talk to the organisers and help to enlarge it.

SUMMARY

- Make sure you work out your festival expenses fully. Do not rely on guessing (and underestimating)
- Make sure you reward sponsors and publicise their involvement

- Hold taster events – you will raise money, attract audiences and promote your festival
- Become a serious networker
- Pricing and selling tickets may well be tricky
- Start early in spreading the word

5

The importance
of budgets

Paul Kelly has devised, programmed, project-managed and staged a wide range of festivals and events, reaching audiences of up to eighty thousand people. These include Soundwaves Rock Festival (Plymouth 1995-98), The Eclipse Festival (Plymouth 1999), two millennium events, the royal golden jubilee celebrations (Plymouth 2002), Plymouth Music Week and the Bournemouth Jazz Festival 2016. In this chapter he explains the intricacies of budgeting and fundraising. If you have a new or small festival then you may simply want to pick and choose what you need. As your festival grows, come back and dip into this section once more.

CREATING YOUR BUDGET

Budgeting for a festival can be a large and complex job, depending on the size of the event. This section can only serve as an introduction.

Planning

Your festival budget plays a key role in translating the excitement of your idea into something that is real and deliverable. Your budget is a key part of your planning process.

What is a budget?

Put very simply, a budget is an estimated list of expenditure (costs) and receipts (income) with a 'bottom line' or 'out-turn' to be filled in after your event. This shows whether or not you have made a profit or a loss – or, as some people like to describe it, a 'surplus' or a 'deficit'.

Purpose

Note the word 'estimated' in the above definition. A budget is your best guess. As such, you are aiming to estimate costs and income to make sure they and you meet your objectives. Make sure you are clear about what your financial objectives are; make sure these dovetail with your overall objectives for the festival and use your budget to help ensure you are meeting them.

Best guesses, estimates and research

When you start putting a budget together, a lot of it will be guesswork. But don't leave it there. You need to turn guesses into reliable figures. That requires research. For example, if you need to hire a hall, lighting, chairs, a generator, portable loos or any one of many things such events often require, then go and get some quotes and turn your guesses into an actual figure. Two or three estimates of the same type of supply will soon give you a feel for this.

But where and how do you get estimates? Organisers of similar events may be able to give you advice. Look at what is going on in your area. Also use *Yellow Pages* or trade directories such as yell.com. Search on categories such as 'staging'. Contact companies and ask for a quote.

Be specific

There is one more thing you may also need to do, before you get quotes. You need to be able to specify what it is you want. When your needs are technical, the more detail you can specify the better. By doing that you are also ensuring you can compare like with like.

Comparing estimates

There are some things that you can get comparable quotes on and there are some things that you simply cannot compare in purely financial terms. A leading exception to the rule about getting comparable quotes is artists and creative suppliers. By and large they are not usually directly comparable – how can you compare a string quartet with a big jazz band? Artists and performers will usually have a set price. That price may be negotiable but it won't normally be directly comparable.

STRUCTURE AND FORMAT

So, you have an outline festival plan. You know whether it's going to be indoors or outdoors (or both), when it's likely to take place, the sort of content you want, who might be interested in it and some of the technical things you might need to make it work.

So, how do you put all this together?

There are several ways of constructing a festival budget. The two I am going to focus on here are 'top-down' and 'bottom-up'.

In the case of top-down you put some headings together (see below), run some estimated figures against them and see how they look. Are you facing a massive loss or a nice, fat profit? Does your proposed event look viable? That can be a quick starting point, but ultimately you will also need a bottom-up approach. That means doing detailed costings on every aspect of your festival – and if you have lots of events in lots of venues, then costings for each one of these. From this you may end up with a very big budget with lots of figures. But it also ought to be a very accurate one.

I strongly recommend you devise your budget using a spreadsheet like Excel. If you use pen and paper, or a word processor, it's more likely to lead to arithmetical errors and it will be far slower to adjust when you make changes – and you will undoubtedly be making lots of changes to your budget!

Budgets and spreadsheets pro-tip

As you will inevitably run through many variations and versions of your budget, keep track of them. Put the date and a version number in the file name of your spreadsheet. When you update the budget, save it under a new name with the latest date and a new file version number. For example – you start with a budget called 'Cliveden Arts Festival budget v1 15 October 2017'. You revise that the following month and then save this new version as 'Cliveden Arts Festival budget v1a 12 November 2017'. This means you always know *precisely* which version you are working from and which is the *latest*.

HOW TO DRAW UP YOUR BUDGET

It doesn't matter whether you start your budget off with income or expenditure, though I prefer to start with income – if nothing else, it focuses the mind on the fact that you need some.

Some people like to put income and expenditure side by side on the page. I recommend you put them one above the other. That way you can easily add extra lines. See the example below. This is the sort of thing you need to include and the figures can be updated monthly.

Opening balance/carried forward

Grant income	£
Sponsorship	£
Individual donations	£
Sub-total	**£**

Box office income

Standard weekend tickets	£
'Early bird' discount tickets	£
Concession tickets	£
Saturday day-tickets	£
Sunday day-tickets	£
Coffee pitch fee	£

Coffee and teas – sales	£
Programme adverts	£
Sub-total	**£**
Total income	**£**

Expenditure

Venue hire	£
Fees	£
Rider [hospitality for performers] expenses	£
Marketing	£
Production costs	£
Stage-dressing	£
Staffing fees	£
Contingency	£
Total expenditure	**£**

CATEGORIES

Budgets can have masses of information and, if you are not careful, you can get lost in the detail. That's why it's important that you structure it into sections. Excel allows you to have as many pages of information as you want and to link these pages. If it's a big and complex event, I find it helps to have a simple opening budget page with totals and then more detailed workings on separate spreadsheet pages. You can clearly see the overview without being overwhelmed by too many numbers.

You can add sub-headings and costs as you go. Here are some examples:

Income

- Box office (or 'earned income')
- Other sales
- Grants
- Commercial sponsorship (or business sponsorship)
- Donations (could include crowdfunding or that could be a separate category)
- Raffle (s)
- Concessions (fees from stallholders)

Expenditure

- Artists fees and costs
- Rider (or 'hospitality' – see below)
- Box office commission (agency fees)
- Venue hire
- Infrastructure (stage, sound, lights, decor)
- Marketing and publicity
- Insurance
- Staffing or organiser costs
- National Insurance (employing permanent staff)
- Volunteer expenses

You might have further sub-headings. For example, under 'marketing' you could break it down by posters and leaflets, press advertising, brochure/programme, public relations, website development, social media advertising, etc. You could list those details on a separate marketing budget page that would be linked to a total marketing figure in your summary, keeping that overall page clean and simple.

EASY READING

You may well end up with a page covered in figures. If you can't read, understand and interpret those figures you and your committee will be in potential difficulty. To make it easier to read, both for you and others, especially if you are using a spreadsheet:

- Get rid of the pence – no one cares about 14p
- If your numbers involve thousands, format the numbers to include a comma so that £1000 reads £1,000
- Put sub-totals in italics and totals in bold; they stand out better

A word of warning

A computerised spreadsheet program like Excel can automatically add up rows or columns and give you a total that updates when you add new data. It's very handy, but if you have sub-totals make sure that they are not included in the final figure. It is all too easy to add up a column of figures that include sub-totals and 'double-count' the figures. If it's on the expenditure side it might not be a disaster. But if you are double-counting income, it could lead to a financial catastrophe.

CONTINGENCY

There will always be costs you can't predict. So it is sensible to put in a contingency budget of whatever you think you can – I would suggest at least five hundred pounds and preferably more if you can. If you have to adjust the budget because you get less in box office income or grants, then your contingency budget provides a useful cushion.

THE RIDER

The artist rider is a list of extras which form part of the contract that event organisers are required to supply for performers. For local or emerging acts, the rider might range from light to non-existent, but a bit of light refreshment will always be appreciated. Well-established acts are likely to have more extensive demands. These can cover the specific supply of equipment, meals, towels and overnight accommodation. Riders can also be negotiated in the contract and, if you can get them right down, you can just ask the guests on the day, 'Is there anything I can get you?' If they feel looked after, their requests will probably be quite modest.

ESTIMATING BOX OFFICE INCOME

This is another big unknown that requires careful thought and judgement. Most festivals involve ticketing and box office income. You will also need to track ticket sales to see if things are going to plan. If they are not, you might need to adjust your marketing and publicity. Selling tickets for festivals involves a range of issues that are worth briefly outlining here as it will help you estimate your income. These issues include:

- The nature of the event
- Fees and expenses to cover

- The kind of audience you hope to attract
- The number of customers you are hoping to attract
- The size of your venue
- Technical and other costs of staging
- Ticket prices for same or similar events
- Ticket outlets
- Your willingness to risk a loss for a 'must-have' star or the need to make money

There may well be other questions you will need ask, that will be specific to your festival and location.

Your ticket pricing and estimates will probably vary by type of event:

- A talk by a children's author
- A concert featuring a rising pop band
- A demonstration by a celebrity chef

In summary, the key points in your budget estimate are:

- How much can/should you charge?
- How many people can your venue hold?
- How potentially popular is your offer?

Never budget on one hundred per cent capacity. Inevitably, you will have to hold back some tickets for guests, VIPs, competition prizes, the press and the like – these are known as complimentary tickets or 'comps'. Normal practice is to budget at seventy per cent capacity. So if you are staging a festival that involves some sort of talk or performance and have a three-hundred-capacity venue and decide to charge fifteen pounds a head and you budget at seventy per cent capacity that means you could expect an income of £3,150. (300 x 70% = 210 x £15 = £3,150). Hold on a second: that assumes that everyone pays full price. Are you going to offer any discounts for older people or children (assuming it's suitable) or other discounts? If you do, make sure you factor them in.

All of this applies to the bottom-up method of budgeting I talked about. This method of budgeting ticket income is also really useful in setting out what you can afford to pay for your speaker or artist or production or attraction. If, say, you have a five-hundred-capacity venue and you budget on seventy per cent capacity, what's your maximum revenue? Well, it all depends on how high you set the ticket price and what people are willing to pay.

There are lots of possible permutations here. Factors include your locality, what competing events are going on and just how much disposable income your audience really has and how much they actually want to see what you are putting on.

Budgeting for box office income – indeed, the whole process of budgeting – is a balancing act full of variables and nuances. Don't let that put you off! It can also be very creative and satisfying.

BOX OFFICE VARIABLES AND ACTUALS

How do you turn all these variables into a sensible set of box office income projections that complete your draft budget? You have to estimate your audience number for each event, multiply that by the ticket price, subtract any discounts you are offering and put the resulting figure in your income column.

You will inevitably want to play around with the figures a bit. A spreadsheet program also allows you to run all sorts of 'what-if' scenarios. For example, what if our audience numbers were ten per cent larger? What if we put the ticket prices up by ten per cent?

CASH FLOW

Budgeting is a key part of ensuring financial success. But there is one other important aspect. You may also have heard of the term 'cash flow'. Cash flow is different from a budget and can save you from disaster.

A budget is a projection – of where your income and costs are likely to come from and what you expect the outcome to be; i.e. how much profit you hope to make. Cash flow is a projection of *when* income will arrive and *when* costs will be payable. Its purpose is to help you ensure you have enough money in the bank at critical times to meet your obligations.

Cash-flow format is like a budget, but stretched over twelve months or possibly a shorter time frame for festivals. The first column in the cash flow should be the estimated budget total. You will then have up to twelve further columns, one for each month. You take your total figure and allocate this to the months when you expect to receive the income or make the payment. The monthly figures will show you how much cash you have or will need to keep your event running. A cash-flow may not in itself solve your problems. But it will tell you where and when they will be and allow you identify ways of meeting your obligations. Like a budget, a cash-flow projection is a dynamic document – only more so. You will need to update it regularly. Expect to revise and update your cash flow monthly and possibly more often.

SUMMARY

- Work within a budget to estimate the money you will need
- Remember the importance of detailed costings and the value of using a spreadsheet
- Don't forget contingency planning and artists' rider costs
- Use those practical ways of estimating your box office income and dealing with your cash flow

6

Assembling a
balanced programme

*A festival should provide something for everyone, for all
ages and for all interests. Make sure you have a variety of
events to suit all tastes.*

PROGRAMME FOR A WIDE AUDIENCE

Make a list of possible speakers or demonstrators for each age
group – children, teenagers, young women, young men, older
and retired people – and put down the names of speakers you
would like to take part. Remember that you won't necessarily
get your first choice and that some of them will be suitable for
everyone.

For example, a literary festival needs:

- Authors of fiction who can be from genres that are literary,
  light-reading, historical, fantasy, crime or thriller
- Authors of non-fiction – biography, history, geography,
  travel, factual, politics, poetry, sport, nature and gardening,
  comedy

If you are organising a literary festival it is important to choose from a variety of genres. You don't want to discover that all your speakers are from one genre unless that is the point – for example, the Chalk Valley History Festival. The main thing is that there should be something for everyone.

In our festival we tried to cover all bases. We had a festival church service on the last Sunday that was full of literary references. So many traditional hymns were written by well-known poets – Christina Rossetti, John Wesley, Alfred Tennyson, George Herbert – and at the other end of the scale we introduced 'Poems in a Pub with a Pint' and invited people to come with something they had written or a poem they particularly liked. At the organising stage this concept proved to be controversial – most of our committee felt that we'd be lucky to get an audience of one man and his dog. Our poetry adviser – very reluctantly – went along to the chosen pub, armed with several poems of his own, and was amazed to find thirty people waiting for him, all clutching their poems. Our town obviously has a collection of closet poets.

Literary pub crawls and literary town tours can also be successful and help to bring your whole area into your festival. I heard Viv Groskop, when she was artistic director of the Independent Bath Literary Festival, say that the whole festival should be like a library that has come to life and feels like a party. That's so true. You have to build an atmosphere of expectation.

If your festival lasts for a few days make sure there are plenty of extras for the crowds. Lydia Brammer of River Cottage Festival agrees. 'There must be enough going on to keep people entertained. Some people will be camping for the whole time so there must be things happening for them to do over a few days and a lot of hidden areas of interest.'

EXPANDING YOUR IDEAS

You want to attract people from outside your town but you must make sure that the residents of the town feel included. Remember the housewives and mums as well as those professional people who can only manage evening and weekend events.

Variety is the spice of a festival.

The people who were in at the beginning of Oundle Festival of Literature (and I was one of them) were thinking well outside the box when they were planning their first events and came up with some interesting ideas. 'We had a community part of the festival where we encouraged people to write and so we had poetry slams and writing competitions,' explains Paula Prince. 'We had workshops and other writing events but we also provided things that perhaps people wouldn't normally go to. For example, I did a writers' salsa and included the local salsa group and a man who had written a book on salsa. He came and read from his book and then we all learned salsa. We did things like that for the community side of the Festival. It was slightly whacky, and then we covered the whole town with poetry, the *whole* town, *everywhere*! People loved it. The idea was to bring in people who wouldn't normally attend a festival or would think that poetry was too highbrow.'

FINDING SPEAKERS AND PERFORMERS

Booking the right people for your festival is an art in itself. You can read much more about it in the following section,

Chapter 7, but let's consider it briefly here first. There are various ways of attracting speakers or performers. One way – which I feel is not professional and is not something I would do – is the personal approach. It may be that you have well-known performers or authors living locally or their friends or relatives and you could consider going directly through them. This is done by quite a few festival organisers and, it has to be said, very successfully. But I believe that you retain greater control over what is going on if you go through their business representatives.

For example, if you are looking for authors to speak at your festival you should be in touch with their publicists. Telephone the publisher and ask who the publicist is for the author. The role of the publicist is crucial in organising book-signings and festival appearances of an author and he or she – most probably she – organises the speaking schedules. For instance, it is a bit impractical for someone to be speaking at an event in Edinburgh one evening and at another in Plymouth the next morning. Publicists will also have biographical information about the author, a note of how far he or she will travel and often the size of audience they expect – and remember, never, ever, exaggerate about the crowd. Be honest, even if you add that you expect more will be coming and paying at the door. People frequently leave their evening plans to the last minute and then just turn up and expect to find seats.

Be professional when booking speakers.

Tanya Bruce-Lockhart also works through publicists. 'I book authors through their publicists and then I get their emails and mobile telephone numbers and I can arrange the logistics of getting them down here,' she says.

Keep it simple

When you are planning your programme, especially for your first festival, try and keep it easy for everyone to follow. Even if it seems too simple to you, it is unlikely to be for your audience, who will not have been involved in planning the programme.

'If I started it again I would make the programme less complicated,' says Emma Fernandez of Purbeck Festival. 'We have run it for two weeks and in 2017 it is shorter but much more diverse. We know what works now.' So don't worry – after your first couple of festivals you will know what works for your audience, your team and the venues.

USE YOUR LOCAL KNOWLEDGE

Remember that the facilities you have around you can work to enhance the festival. This is how the organisers of the River Cottage Festival diversified to give the visitors what they wanted.

'For the first time ever we are opening River Cottage farmhouse as a restaurant where people can just walk in and have a meal,' says Lydia Brammer of the 2016 event. 'That means visitors to the festival can have a River Cottage experience without having to book beforehand, although they will need festival tickets to come in. We have a company coming in showing children circus skills, we have bushcraft workshops and wood workshops. We have made sure there are a lot of things for children of all ages.'

It's important to step back and take an objective view of the festival and what you want it to be. This is hard to do if it's your first festival but as you do more, so you begin to know what works within your parameters and what your visitors like. Dorchester Literary Festival organisers worked this out when they brought the life and work of author Thomas Hardy into their festival.

'We have a Thomas Hardy event that's slightly different from other festivals,' says Janet Gleeson. 'The Thomas Hardy Society wanted to be involved in the Festival. We didn't want it to be an academic lecture so we had this idea of asking contemporary writers to discuss a theme relating to Hardy and, whether wittingly or unwittingly, they felt that Hardy had influenced their own work. We have a walk in Thomas Hardy country and because of the rural aspect of our location we are offering a whole day at the local agricultural college. Everything is linked to the theme of the countryside including all the books.'

BE INCLUSIVE

A festival should be for everyone unless you are organising an exclusively themed one. An opera festival would attract lovers of classical music as well as keen opera fans. You need to get your whole community behind you because, although you want people from further away, local people will have friends and family who will want to come along. This is something Paula Prince strongly supports.

'You need to have something that appeals to everyone,' she says. 'I made sure that there was something for three-year olds and something for ninety-three-year olds and something for everyone in between. We used to take the festival into the residential homes. It was mainly performance poetry. I used to go into these homes four or five weeks beforehand and get people writing poetry. We always found that poetry was very popular with the elderly. They used to love monologues and we found an eighty-eight-year-old lady who did the most incredible monologues.'

Contact local clubs and societies, mother and toddler groups, schools and day care centres and find out what they would like to have at a festival. You may be able to recruit some helpers, too.

STEADY AS YOU GO

As useful as it is to have ideas and suggestions for your festival there is really only one person who can put together the programme and that has to be the organiser. You need that overall viewpoint to ensure balance and a certain amount of uniformity. It is also important not to let two potentially popular events clash, something which happened to me. We had a top author coming to give a talk and, after our programme was printed, we discovered the local library had a similar event. Try as we might, there was no way we could change the times and people were very put out. The following year, we included both authors in our programme and had full houses. Both authors were accomplished speakers and people were happy to hear them again.

Kenneth Richardson, of Oundle International Festival, is another who retains oversight of the festival: 'I do the programming, which is difficult because you have to get it balanced,' he says. 'It's about getting to know the audience but also trying to persuade them to try something slightly different and to experiment. I try to encourage people not just to come to the things they *think* they'll like but to try something they think they might not have wanted to go to.' Do have contrasts and encourage diversity in your programme. Don't put on similar acts back to back and make sure your line-up of speakers, acts, artists, demonstrators or musicians is inspiring!

'Variety', 'inspirational', 'balance' and 'appealing to all' are the buzzwords.

A GLOSSY LOOK

You need to find a good graphic designer for your programme. Discuss with him or her exactly what you want and how you see the finished programme. The designer will make sensible suggestions based on experience and it is worth listening because what you want may not necessarily be right for your programme or could end up looking inappropriate or dull when it is translated into print. So don't be intransigent; build up a good working relationship with your designer.

The cover

The cover of the programme is important. You want it to stand out and be immediately recognisable. So choose the colours carefully and have a design that is clear even from a distance.

Logo or no go

Have you got an image or an illustration that immediately identifies your festival? Your designer can devise several for you to consider. The simpler the better and, ideally, using not more than two colours. Take your time deciding what you want and remember, something that is *almost* right can be tweaked. The finished article will be part of your branding and you should be able to use it every year. It will go on your letterheads, your invitation cards – in fact, anything to do with the festival. As soon as someone spots that sign they will know that what they will be reading involves your festival, including all posters and flyers.

Famous photos

Contact the agents or publicists of your well-known acts or speakers and ask for quality colour images. Ideally, they should be digital, colour and 300 dpi. Not only will their shots illustrate the text in the programme but you can print them off and use them as part of your advertising and publicity (see chapter 8).

Short and sweet

Do not write five hundred words about one act and 150 about another. Assuming the size of your programme is A5 (around 15 cm by 21 cm), you should try and keep the text down to two hundred words for each act. Include the title, the date, the time and the venue. Make your text sizzle! Write some-thing that will encourage people to buy tickets and do make sure it is in clear type. Some older people have trouble reading small type and designers have a habit of using tints and pale print. The programme is supposed to inform your potential audience. It should not irritate because it is attractive but very hard to read.

Calling all *Mad Men*

Some festivals prefer not to include advertising but I recommend it; the revenue adds up and it can pay for the design and printing of the programme. Advertisements can either be at the end of the programme or within the editorial pages. Try to keep a tidy look with advertisements making full or half-pages.

Information overload

Pack out your programme. You need a map showing venues as well as a list of sponsors, advertisers and supporters, alongside the daily diary. List everything. For example, if you have a pop-up café, give the opening times, where it is located and what it serves. If you have a writer-in-residence, an artist-in-residence, a musician or a cookery demonstrator, someone showing how to make scarecrows or hats, explain when and where they will be during the festival. Your programme should also feature:

- any agreed discounts and addresses of local restaurants, cafés or B&Bs
- an overview of every event – including date, time, venue and ticket pricing
- details of how to purchase tickets and a booking form with another list of all events and prices and a space for the

purchaser's name and telephone number in case an event is cancelled and you need to return money

- the date of the next year's festival – which should be at roughly the same time

For your first festival, you may not want to go to all the trouble of producing a full programme. You can get away with a sheet of A4 paper (29.5cm x 21cm) folded into three sections with a small image of each performer and around fifty words of blurb. Don't forget the front cover section with your logo, dates of the festival, a few of the top names and where to buy tickets. It's easy and cheaper than a fully designed programme and does the same job as a flyer.

SUMMARY

- Plan events for all ages
- Confirm speakers and performers in a professional manner
- Don't be selective – involve the whole community
- Think up a wide variety of events

7

Choosing contributors and stallholders

It is a fact of life that even the most brilliant of writers may be a hopeless public speaker. Just because someone can write well doesn't mean they can speak as fluently, engagingly or knowledgeably as they write. In fact, between you and me, many are seriously boring.

LISTEN AND LOOK BEFORE YOU BOOK

It is very important to hear everyone you are about to engage for your festival speak before you book them. The same applies to musicians – hear them play – and demonstrators and stallholders – you must see them before you book them. Find out where authors are speaking at other festivals and make a point of going to hear them. It is not just their ability to engage an audience but the content of their talk that is important.

Paul Kelly has been involved in finding artistes, acts and bands for many years. He makes the following points:

- At a local level, there are lots of local musicians around – check out your regional newspapers and online. Go for who you like and who you think would be good value. Talk to other people about them. Do remember that if they are performing locally for free, they may not bring audiences because everybody knows them already.

- Classical – there are lots of classical agents out there with loads of people on their books. They would be happy to sell you a quartet.
- There are lots of similar agents in jazz, although many musicians prefer to be booked direct. Agencies handle the larger ones but check jazz publications too and look online. Try *The Jazz Guide* (www.thejazzguide.co.uk) which has been going for over forty years and lists jazz events, bands and venues.
- The rock and pop world is a lot harder because it's popular and in a funny sort of way it's harder to access. There are agents there as well but the really high-profile acts tour at particular times of the year and you would be lucky to get a look in.
- Smaller groups can be a good alternative – it's a question of looking further down the lists at other festivals and not just at headliners. Most bands have a website and contact address details.

TALENT-SCOUTING

'The main acts are the most popular,' says James Shepard of the Larmer Tree Festival, 'and people like discovering a band they have never heard of. We put on something like eighty or ninety music acts at the festival. There are a million ways in which we choose the line-up. Sometimes it's to do with who we've booked and trying to get the balance of music. And it's getting out there and listening to music. We have lots of agents who we are constantly talking to and they are talent-scouting for us in a way. They are pitching literally hundreds and hundreds of acts to us and we have to whittle them down to something that we feel we are looking for. The only way of *really* finding out is to go and see a band. You can listen to music and watch videos but in the end it's the relationship between the band and the audience.'

HOW TO CONTACT AN AUTHOR

As we touched on in the previous chapter, it is best to contact an author through their publicist although there are still some festival organisers who go directly to a speaker. Author Jane Corry, who was brought in to help at Sidmouth Literary Festival, looks at things differently. 'My experience was all rather last-minute,' she explains. 'I was put in charge of finding authors because I have the most contacts. One of the things I really learnt is that sometimes cold-calling can work but sometimes it doesn't. For example, I tracked down Terry Waite's publicist, not expecting him to reply and he did, saying that he would come to the festival. That was after several weeks of leaving messages for other authors and not getting anywhere. I think the lesson there is aim high because even those who are very much in the public eye will respond. I learnt not to take umbrage if people don't get back to me. People have so much going on when they are published authors and can't always keep up with all the incoming emails. A phone call can be better than an email.

'If I can go through the author, I do. Sometimes a personal connection beats anything else. And sometimes the message gets through faster. They may well say, "You need to approach my publicist." If you know somebody who *knows* somebody, then that helps. I knew quite a lot of people who offered to send a personal email or make a phone call. There were a few people I chased and chased. They would say they'd do their best or ask me to ring them in a couple of months. I have learnt that I wouldn't contact them again after the third approach. There were a few I did because they actually led me to believe they might take part in the festival and then they didn't at the last minute. I found that rather frustrating.'

Be persistent but don't expect every invitation to be accepted.

Janet Gleeson had a lucky break. 'There was one person who gave us advice when we started our festival, and she was a publicist with a large publisher,' she says. 'She told us how to approach the speakers. She said what you needed to do was get a few well-known names under your belt and then when you have got them, write to all the publicists in London and explain we were starting a new festival, these people were already on board and they will be a magnet to attract others. That's exactly what we did. She suggested December was a good month to do this as publicists were not that busy. Again, we were lucky because my writing background and Paul's writing background meant we had various contacts. I knew Tracy Chevalier was living in the area as was Minette Walters so we approached them and other people and, without exception, they all said, "Yes, we'd like to be part of it."'

Take advice from people who understand your contributors' business, be it music, publishing, food, etc.

Jane Corry believes in talking to people before they are invited to take part in a festival. 'If you are organising your own festival I think it's a good thing to talk to people and also listen to speakers. They may have a big name but not be great at speaking. They might be better at running a workshop.'

Paula Prince agrees. She believes personal contact is the best way to get an author to come along to a festival. 'The nice thing about Oundle's festival was that it was a very personal festival,' she says. 'We really looked after our authors and we fed them extremely well – they always had a lovely dinner to go to afterwards. They used to say that they liked coming to Oundle because it was such a nice atmosphere.' Apparently, there was always an interesting variety of sandwiches in the Green Room at Oundle but it seems the authors liked the chocolate 'Krispy Kakes' best of all!

TO PAY OR NOT TO PAY

I think that now there are so many festivals, the speakers or performers should always be offered a fee. If the bar staff, cleaners and technicians get paid, then so should the main attraction. This is a tricky decision, though, because many small festivals run on a shoestring in the early years. None of the organisers are paid and many do not take expenses. They argue that authors are usually plugging a new book and will get royalties from books sold or that bands love to have an opportunity to perform. In my view that is rather a naïve point of view. Not every member of an audience will buy a book and often book sales are very low.

> Think honestly about the best performers travelling to your festival for nothing.

It's true that in many music festivals there are new bands who do not demand a fee but welcome the opportunity to play. Helen Stickland is a vocalist and guitar player in a three-piece band called Design. 'We are paid for a few gigs but we often do a gig as a favour and also to get more exposure,' she says. 'We were invited to take up two slots at the New York Indy Pop Festival in 2016 and both gigs went well and were sold out so we are hoping to be invited back. We were paid although we had to make our own way there but there was still some money left over.'

Fees proved a tricky point for Janet Gleeson. 'One of the first important decisions we had to make was whether we were going to pay the speakers,' she says. 'We decided that we would and I think that was the right thing to do. The Society of Authors recommends a fee of £150-250 so that was what we decided to pay. But as soon as you decide that, you are incurring expenses which you have not necessarily anticipated. Paul Atterbury and I were going to fund the festival ourselves and put in five hundred each but as soon as we realised we had to pay speakers as well we knew we needed to get sponsors. It helped that the local auctioneer offered us space to hold the talks free of charge and so did the museum.'

Oundle Festival of Literature paid slightly under the amount suggested by the Society of Authors. 'We never paid an author more than a hundred pounds because they usually had a book out to sell and they were "on the circuit",' explains Paula Prince. 'How it worked was we used to try to marry up a really well-known author with one that was up and coming so it would be like a double bill. We also tried to have one really hard-hitter that would make money so we had something in the bank for the start of the festival next year. We had people like Rageh Omah or Kate Adie or Paddy Ashdown – people like that.'

Tanya Bruce-Lockhart of Bridport Festival explains how she deals with payment. 'I find the speakers, negotiate with their publicists or sometimes with their agents. Up until two years ago we didn't pay our speakers because that seemed to be de rigueur with literary festivals. But there has been such a growth of festivals that it seemed unfair to expect an author to come all the way to Bridport and not be paid. The publishers simply can't afford to underwrite them all the time. What I feel comfortable about now is all our writers get paid and we cover their travel expenses and their accommodation. We give them a good time and we make them feel appreciated. Local people often give dinner parties for some of the authors after their events.'

One author I spoke to was still smarting over her treatment. 'One festival rescinded on their agreement to pay for my overnight accommodation and travel expenses, due to "poor ticket sales" for my event. They'd sold forty-eight tickets at £16.50 a head in a venue that would have held only a few more people – I make that nearly £800 gross. I did a return car journey of six hours, spoke for two hours and forked out £160 for the privilege. The organiser was shameless.'

You can imagine that this author is going to tell anyone and everyone about her treatment. Would she advise another author to take part in a future festival organised by the same people?

Make sure you do not alienate performers – always honour agreements.

To pay or not to pay is not so clear cut at the River Cottage Festival. 'It depends on what they see is fair,' says Lydia Brammer. 'If they have an agreement to stay in the hotel and have three nights' accommodation and dinner every night, then that is taken into consideration.'

As you see, it can be a really thorny problem. 'I think you have to pay authors these days,' says Jane Corry. 'I have been to some festivals where you have the option of saying you don't mind not accepting a fee. You can look at that in two ways; it's a good idea but the author can feel obliged to not accept a fee. At Sidmouth we had three authors who very kindly said they didn't want a fee. Some festivals have a little box that you can tick if you don't want to take a fee. This is something we are considering but the only thing that worries me is that authors might feel obliged to tick it.'

SEARCH FOR A STAR

It is not wise to get too many people out looking for the talent. Suggestions of names and recommendations are important but there should be only *one* person, the festival organiser, who makes the final decision. To be professional, the speaker, band or workshop leader has to understand they are making a serious commitment. People are well meaning and try to be helpful and if someone offers to make contact, this contact should be followed up. Too often you are likely to hear that someone's daughter's best friend is related to just the person you need for the festival. Let them make the contact and find out if this person is free on the date you need them. The organiser then takes over.

Imagine the scene: a gathering of friends chatting and one says, 'We are having a festival this year. It would be great if you could come with your puppet show.' The person, or puppeteer, agrees to take part and to many people that is the job done. But it's not. It is just the beginning. Does that puppeteer realise the commitment he or she has made? The event will be put in the festival programme, tickets will be sold, the venue booked and other similar events will be refused. If they pull out there will be a gap that will take a lot of work to fill. Too often these gaps are left until the last minute and that has people running round unnecessarily.

MAKING A CONTRACT

When you engage a contributor you need to give them a contract so that there is no confusion over what is expected. Apart from providing useful information so that the speaker knows exactly what will happen and what he or she should know about the festival, it formalises what might have been a request to take part. The contract does not have to be complicated but must state the facts and can be in the form of a letter (see Appendix for a typical contract letter).

TAKE CARE OF THE TALENT

One of the worst things you can do is leave your guests to get on with things on their own. Once the contracts are signed, it is time to start cosseting them. Each one must feel they are the most important person taking part in the festival – and the likelihood is that they are. Email them about a month before the start to say how much you are looking forward to their arrival. Assign someone to look after them. Each one needs a chaperone or minder and this is an important task because that person is, in effect, representing your festival (see also the next heading). They must never be left on their own unless they specifically ask to be. One of the worst things you can do is abandon an author.

There are some gruesome tales. I remember booking one very well-known author whose publicist I knew quite well. A few days before the event the publisher rang me and asked what arrangements we had made. It is very unusual for a publisher to get involved with a festival booking but I thought nothing more about it and explained that he would be met at the station, taken to the hotel, then picked up to go to the venue. The morning he was due to arrive I had four or five calls from his train. The author was not travelling with his publicist but with someone else and this person, who I assumed was another publicist, was asking very basic questions:

'Will we be met at the station?'

'Yes.'

'He likes to see the venue first.'

'No problem. You can go to the hotel via the venue.'

'Is there a clock at the venue?'

'Yes.'

'He will want a glass of still water on stage.'

'We always have a carafe of water for our speakers.'

'Will someone collect him from the hotel and take him to the venue and after his talk take him back to the hotel?'

'Of course. There is always someone with our speakers and they are taken back to their hotels.'

I discovered that a few weeks earlier this author had been at a festival and was duly met and looked after and taken to the venue to give his talk. He had a successful book-signing and when the last person had gone there was no one around to take him back to the hotel. He was in a strange town, it was a Sunday night, he hadn't eaten and all the restaurants were closed. He had no idea where he was and was not best pleased. I discovered the man who had accompanied him to our festival and made all the telephone calls to me was the managing director of the publishing house. Always make sure that speakers have a chaperone or minder who *never* leaves a speaker's side until they are delivered to their mode of transport home.

We had an author whose event was scheduled for eight o'clock on a wet and windy October night. She only lived some thirty miles away, but it was a difficult drive through narrow country lanes. She came directly to the venue, arriving at around six-thirty and by that time she was in a very bad temper. We offered her a drink – tea, coffee or wine – and something to eat from our pop-up café. She began to calm down and was pleasantly surprised when she asked to see the hall and try out her PowerPoint presentation to learn we had our technician on hand and that everything she needed to use actually worked! After her talk, which was very well received, she hugged us and thanked us for making the event go so smoothly for her – something she was not expecting when she arrived.

Our worst experience happened during our very first festival. It was on the last day and all was going well; we had managed to cope successfully with the problems that had arisen (and believe me, there were various crises and near disasters that first year). We were pleased that we had managed to get through the festival and we were all feeling very relieved that nothing terrible had happened. And then *Private Eye* ran a column about the festival.

It seems that one of our speakers was a convicted paedophile and what was worse his event had taken place on school premises. This was at the time when the Jimmy Savile scandal was at its height and so I was getting telephone calls from local and national newspapers and radio stations. I was so relieved that I could say, hand on heart, that this person had a member of the festival team with him at all times, that the event was in the evening and, despite being on school premises, there were no children present. What a thing to happen at your first festival! Yet, it showed that we were absolutely right in insisting that speakers are accompanied. That does not mean that you will have a similar situation but it does show that you have to be prepared for any eventuality.

A member of your team should accompany your talent at all times.

At our first festival, one of our committee members was looking after a speaker but had to leave at the end of the talk. She told a friend to watch the speaker, but this new chaperone had no idea where to take the speaker or what to do. It could have turned into a difficult situation but was saved by committee members discovering what had happened and taking over. It is proof that you must brief people fully.

The same rules apply across the board. Make sure performers are relaxed and happy at your festival, whether authors, other kinds of speakers or groups or workshops.

GUIDELINES FOR CHAPERONING SPEAKERS

Authors must have someone they can turn to for help AT ALL TIMES. If they want something to eat or drink, if they need the loo, if they want to see the town, if they want to shop, there *must* be someone there to show them. This is imperative because you want them to leave the festival having had a very enjoyable experience. Here is a summary of the key points:

- Make sure the chaperones know how their VIP is arriving: train, bus, car or whatever. If it is by train, get them to meet on the platform. If by car, make sure they know where they are parking.
- The chaperone needs to know how long before the event the guest needs to be at the venue. Factor in time for sound-checks, etc.
- Allow time to take the guests to the green room to meet the person who will be introducing them and who will take over. Offer them a drink or a snack.
- Chaperones should be available during the talk – at literary festivals, especially when the author goes to sign books, as this can often resemble a scrum!
- After any signing it may be that the author has to catch a train so the chaperone's job is to keep an eye on the clock to make sure he or she gets to the station on time. They may have to extricate them from fans!
- The guest has to get back to the car or the station and if they have to wait for a train, the helper has to stay with them unless they insist not. They need to see the guest safely leaving the town.

- If there are any issues chaperones feel they cannot deal with, make sure you are around to help.
- Should the chaperone be called away for any reason, they should tell the organiser or the festival secretary who should take over. They should not simply tell a friend or any other member of the audience who will not know the schedule.
- Chaperones can take their cue from the author. They may want to chat or be quiet before the talk. They may want space to think or they may be very chatty and want to talk.

THE GREEN ROOM

Do not underestimate the importance of a 'green room'. The green room is the name given to the area where authors or demonstrators can relax and gather their thoughts before an event. They will often return there after an event and it needs to be as close as close as possible to the venue where the event is taking place. It is where sponsors can meet the speaker, where the local paper can do an interview and where the person who is introducing the speaker can chat to him or her and find out a bit more about them.

Some speakers bring their partners or spouses with them and one of our speakers brought his pregnant dog because he was worried she might start to give birth when he was away. I was worried too – that she might start to give birth when he was on stage as he insisted on taking her with him. Fortunately, she was very good and sat at his feet while he spoke and we had water waiting for both of them after the event.

Make your green room as attractive as possible. I have been in some very depressing ones, down in the basement of a theatre, for instance, with poor lighting, hard chairs and a miserable ambience. We have brightened very dreary rooms with comfortable chairs, rugs, flowers, books and, of course, tea and coffee-making equipment, water – still and sparkling – and wine. Ask around and there is always someone to lend the odd chair or rug.

Some authors may not drink wine but the fact that it is available gives the impression that we have tried to provide something for everyone – which we have. One of our authors polished off a whole bottle and I think might have started on a second one. That was fine because he Facebooked and tweeted constantly about what a wonderful festival we were and how everyone who is asked should come along to it! That alone was worth a bottle of wine. Remember to have a platter of fruit and interesting biscuits available.

The green room plays a significant part in an author's assessment of a festival. Many guests have told me, a little wistfully, about amazing green rooms that have sides of fresh salmon and whisky on hand for the authors, seriously comfortable armchairs, computers and wi-fi! We couldn't provide anything like that and I assumed that these were festivals that had the backing of large businesses with plenty of money. It made me wonder, in fact, if a festival is mainly judged by the standard of its green room. Our green rooms were always as attractive and welcoming as we could make them. There are some I have visited that were obviously an afterthought, and don't think that goes unnoticed.

SUMMARY

- See potential guests in action before you engage them for your festival. Meet demonstrators and stallholders before you book them

- Use agents to talent-scout for you if you can to get something you are really looking for
- Contact authors for a literary festival through their publicist. Personal connections speed up the process
- Assume that you will be paying authors. Most expect a fee
- Draw up contracts and information sheets so that there is no confusion over what is expected. Look after your speakers so that each feels they are the most important person taking part in the festival. Ensure they are accompanied at all times

8

Marketing, public relations and publicity

Good public relations and publicity are crucial for the success of your festival. That mean much more than just sending a couple of paragraphs about it to your local news-paper, putting an announcement in a local magazine or adding it to a newsletter. People forget.

MAKING AN ANNOUNCEMENT

Posters and flyers

People forget dates unless they put them in their diaries imme-diately (and how many people do that?). The truth is that your exciting bit of information will be bumped out of memory with the next interesting piece of news that comes their way.

Announce your festival with a story in the local paper or the local listings magazine by all means, but also hold an event to get people talking. You can launch with a lively lunch or a smart dinner or even a fish-and-chip supper. Make sure you promote the launch with posters and flyers. The flyers can be one-third of the size of a sheet of A4 paper so they are not expensive. You can do these yourself on a computer and cut the paper into three using the cheapest paper you can get.

Then you put them *everywhere*:

- libraries
- doctor, hospital, vet and dentist waiting rooms
- pubs, cafés, restaurants
- hairdressers and beauty salons
- council offices
- bus and rail stations
- Citizen's Advice Bureaux
- laundrettes

Leave them anywhere that people congregate and have to wait. Ask local shops if they will put some on their counters near the till. Some shops will add a flyer to a bag in which they have wrapped a customer's purchase.

Target places carefully. If you are having a music festival, don't forget to talk to the owner of your local music shop; if it's a literary festival, then go to your bookshops; if it's a food festival, leave flyers where people buy food. The same applies to posters. Ask permission to put them up where people are likely to be waiting and maybe getting bored. If you put enough about and people keep seeing them they are more likely to remember – and buy a ticket. You need to attract the attention of people so that the event, the date and the time stay in their mind.

> If you want people to come to your event then you have to tell them . . . and tell them . . . and then . . . tell them again.

Shout it from the rooftops

It is worth investing in a banner displaying the festival name and the dates. Getting the permissions sorted can be quite a performance so start early if you decide to go for it. You want it hung across a main street. Make sure you check where banners of other events are hung. Then you can go to the owners of the two buildings on which it will be secured and ask permission to put up your banner. Now approach the highways department of the county or unitary council to get permission. Once all this is agreed you need to get someone to deal with the physical work of putting up the banner. There is usually a person who does this so it is just a case of asking around. A number of firms make banners but shop around because the price can vary enormously. Try to get a banner where you can change the date each year rather than having to buy new ones for every festival. That will save you a lot of money.

PRESS RELEASES

A press release is an announcement to all local media – radio, television, newspapers. Send them a good two or three weeks before you expect them to appear as they will need to plan their content. You can embargo your news; in other words, specify that it not be released to the general public until a certain date.

Spend time polishing what you want to say and keep it snappy. It should be carefully thought through and not take up more than one side of a piece of A4 paper. If it looks as though it is going to be a few lines onto another page, try narrowing the margins, which often does the trick. Do not use several fancy fonts or different colours. These are very irritating for a journalist so keep to one clear font such as Bookman Old Style, Arial or Garamond. Steer away from the really fancy ones such as Comic Sans MS, Franklyn Gothic and Matura. You have to look serious. If you are unsure, then stick with Calibri; that is standard on computers although I find it too tight. Think about the size of the typeface. Make it big enough to read easily but not so big that it takes too much space. Twelve or fourteen point usually works for the body of the piece and sixteen or eighteen point for the heading.

A well-written press release is useful for journalists but also helps festival organisers sharpen their message and will highlight the strengths of your festival.

You need to give the information in the inverted pyramid structure, with the bulk in the first paragraph. Expand on this in the next couple of paragraphs. Add quotes from sponsors and include interesting facts behind the festival's creation. Although it seems obvious, don't forget to put in the dates of your festival, the venues, and locations where people can buy tickets. Remember to include your website address.

Press releases can also be posted online. There are a number of free, online distribution services. These make it easy to link with social media and give you even wider exposure. It is worth remembering that it is a useful resource to add to your own festival website under the news section so that journalists and potential festival-goers can read about what's happening in the build-up to the event.

Remember the tried and tested journalists' mantra for ensuring you have included all relevant information – ask, 'who?', 'what?', 'when?', 'where?', 'why?' and 'how?'

Include contact details of more than one person for the journalists' use rather than for publication. Newspapers and radio stations work fast and need information at very short notice. If the one person who can give this is not available they are likely to move on to something else. Contact details should include landline and mobile phone details, email address and home or business address. If the press release doesn't appear in the next issue of the publication or you hear nothing from a radio station, send it again and again. Some people fail to appreciate that a journalist's life can be pretty hectic at times and things get lost.

Finally, give your press release a lively, newsworthy title, something that stands out and that will divert the journalist from all the other press releases they receive every day. Plan a series of press releases spread over the months leading up to the festival. Each one could highlight a different event, a range of personalities or the sponsors.

Be inventive and consistent with a series of press releases.

Get to know your local reporters and talk to them about the festival. They may be able to do a special feature. Ask to see the editor and take along a press pack (see next heading). This should include an overview of the festival, broken down into separate events. Try to include photographs of those people who will be taking part. Give as much information as you can. Journalists have to work fast to a deadline and do not have the time to research.

PREPARING A PRESS PACK

A basic press pack should include the following

Front page
- Cover/front page with logo
- Name of festival
- Dates (always include the names of the days as well as the date)

Page 1
- The organiser and the team details
- Contact numbers
- Photographs

Page 2
- Why you decided to start a festival
- Why this is a good place to hold it
- A brief description of the town and its main features
- Demographics
- Other successful events that take place
- Anything that could appeal to a visitor
- Photographs

Page 3
- What you can offer:
- Venues and capacity
- Refreshment venues
- Green room details
- Technical details: for example, whether microphones – fixed, hand-held and attached – are in all the venues

Page 4
- Accommodation available for visitors
- Illustrate with photographs

Page 5
- How to get to the town by train and car
- How guests are chaperoned
- Comments/quotes/testimonials/endorsements

If you are approaching local monthly magazines, send a press pack three to four months ahead of the festival. Do not be shy about sending your press packs to the nationals, either. You never know when there is a last-minute space to fill where information about your festival would fit nicely.

> Only target relevant periodicals; a music magazine will find little use for news about a hat festival.

START SPREADING THE WORD

Telephone your local radio and TV stations and tell them what you are doing. They are always hungry for news and if they ask you to come and talk about the festival, make sure you take with you a list of things you want to say. It can be daunting to sit in front of a microphone in a small room, and you don't want to dry up. When the red light comes on with the words On Air, it is so easy to freeze and forget anything you ever knew about the festival. Think about what you will say carefully because you want the listeners to be excited by the idea of a festival. Then just relax and talk to the interviewer as if he or she is an old friend and you are just chatting. These radio journalists are so good at putting people at their ease and if you do go quiet they will fill in the gap so it is barely noticeable.

Talk to groups

Offer to give talks to clubs and societies whose members may be interested – the Women's Institute, the Rotary and Probus clubs, for example. Visit mother and toddler groups, schools, youth clubs. Above all, make the forthcoming festival sound exciting – because it will be – and something that no one will want to miss.

'When we first started, publicity was a problem,' says Janet Gleeson, 'but we have now got good contacts with local radio and local television and the local press. In the run-up to the first festival we distributed leaflets extensively because we didn't have a budget for advertising, and publicity and public relations were our main way of reaching out to people. We have a sponsor paying for banners to put across the road. We make sure we have public liability insurance that covers us against any accident that might happen.'

> You don't need to spend a lot of money to get the news out.

Publishers are very supportive when their authors are taking part in a festival. Ask them for storyboards. These are large boards, usually black, with standing supports on the back, that have the name of the festival, the date, a picture of the author and the latest book jacket, the date and time of the event and any other relevant information. Many shops are willing to have one or more of these in their windows before and during the festival.

TOP TIPS FROM THE PROS

Jane Adkins, who runs her own PR company, A Head for PR, writes about her approach to publicising a festival:

Over the years we have helped initiate, create, market and publicise many different festivals aimed at a whole range of audiences. Sometimes the idea can be born out of an issue. A few years ago the folk at Visit South Devon were trying to think of ways to attract more visitors to the region. This was just before Hugh Fearnley-Whittingstall created his sustainable fish campaign.

Through talking to another celebrity chef, Mitch Tonks, we discovered that much of the crab caught in South Devon was being shipped abroad rather than being enjoyed by the local populace and visitors to the region. And with that, the idea of the South Devon Crab Festival was born. In six short months the "Let's Get Cracking" campaign reached a national and regional audience of more than ten million consumers. How did we do it? This is a great example of the power of PR . . .

Armed with some facts and statistics we approached television's most-watched factual TV programme, BBC's *Countryfile* – with an audience of an estimated five million viewers – and, fortunately for us, they loved the idea! Not only did they cover the story about sustainability and the innovative street festival – which featured a long trestle table full of local people, visitors to Dartmouth and one or two celebrities from the area – but the next year we had presenters Clare Balding and Matt Baker coming down to Dartmouth to take part in a crab-picking competition. It also helped that celebrity chef Mitch Tonks, from the Seahorse and Rockfish restaurants in Dartmouth, put his weight behind the festival and brought in some of his celebrity chums for support.

We also had some international support the following year when the Australian celebrity chef Bill Granger featured south Devon crab as part of a documentary for the Good Food Channel. However, if you don't have a well-known celebrity who is willing to put their weight behind your festival, try thinking out of the box:

- Who has made the news (in a good way!) in your area recently?
- Is there a local hero who would be happy to be involved with your plans?
- Is there a local business headed up by an owner who is well known in the area and would love to champion your cause?
- Can you link the festival to fundraising for a local charity to create a good angle for media coverage?

Media coverage

And speaking of media coverage – how does that happen? In the case of the South Devon Crab Festival we produced several press releases and made calls and sent email pitches to journalists writing for key magazines – always ensuring we spoke about the festival and highlighting all the different events and initiatives happening around it. The result was that the South Devon Crab Festival was featured in the *Sunday Times Style*, *BBC Good Food*, *Waitrose Weekend*, *Good Housekeeping* and *BBC Countryfile* magazine as well as in a wide range of travel and trade press. It was also featured extensively in the regional press, including the

Western Morning News, Devon Life and both ITV West Country and BBC TV *Spotlight*. BBC Radio Devon also featured the story as well as attending the launch in Dartmouth in June.

If you are reading this and thinking, that's all very well, but they are a *professional* PR agency, I would like to point out that it is really just a case of doing the research into the media, targeting the right publications and ensuring you have a good story to tell!

As a result of the increased sales in south Devon crab locally and the media interest in the story, the Visit South Devon website experienced a thirty per cent increase in web traffic during the campaign. The tourism partnership made the South Devon or Dartmouth Crab Festival a permanent fixture of the tourism calendar in south Devon and it has gone from strength to strength.

Using social media

Facebook and Twitter can be very useful in creating a buzz around your event and people increasingly use mobile technology – much more so than when we were involved with the crab festival. Don't make the same mistake as another festival with which we were involved recently. They planned their launch and we got them in all the local papers, specialist magazines and on the radio only to learn that the online booking service wasn't going live until several weeks after the launch. There was nowhere that anyone could purchase tickets! What a waste of publicity and effort! Here are some online ideas:

- Use a simple but effective, responsive website that works on your desktop computer as well as your mobile.
- Online booking will need to be set up at the same time as you design your website to make buying tickets as easy as possible.
- Set up Facebook pages and accounts on Twitter, Instagram and YouTube. Most people have a smart-phone that can make a short video. Use it to post across social media.
- Interview your acts, food producers and authors and post tantalising snippets across your social media accounts.
- Set up social media competitions to win tickets to your events.

Specialist media and the national press

If you are organising a food festival, then make sure you contact *all* the specialist consumer-based food magazines well before the event so that it can at least feature in their diary or events pages. If it's a jazz or music festival, then look out for those publications – many of the specialist magazines are monthly or even quarterly. This means they will have long lead times and you need to tell them several months in advance if you are to stand a chance of getting any mentions.

Don't dismiss the national press. All of the main newspapers like *The Times*, the *Guardian*, the *Daily Telegraph* and the *Financial Times* have leisure sections in which they look at what to do at the weekend and any new and interesting events. Go out and buy them and do your research. Find out who is writing about what and send them an email. It is pretty easy to find journalists' email addresses or sometimes a pitch can be better received if you use social media. Time your approach correctly and be very precise about what it is you are telling them and why their particular readership would be interested.

Finding a good photographer

One last piece of advice: don't underestimate the power of images. Make sure you have someone who can take some really good photographs of your festival. These will be useful to post online during the festival to inspire others to come along and join in all the fun.

Those same photographs will be indispensable all over again when it comes to the second year of festival planning. You can do a much better job with your publicity, PR and marketing if you have a bank of excellent photos and videos, something that so many people forget.

> Anyone can take photos on their smartphones, but make sure yours are high resolution images (more than 300 dpi) to be of any use in marketing material or the press.

These are just a few of the things you need to consider on the PR side of promoting a festival. It goes without saying (and, of course, I am going to say it!) that if you need any help, please do get in touch with us at A Head for PR. We love festivals – whether it's planning them, publicising them or even rolling around in the mud at one of the best-known festivals of them all!

SUMMARY

- Make sure you put posters and flyers everywhere
- A banner across a main shopping area reminds everyone of the festival dates
- Devise a fully comprehensive press pack for the media
- Press releases are a vital source of information
- Do use any of the tricks that helped the South Devon Crab Festival become a huge success

9
Solving problems

*Even with the best will in the world and very detailed plan-
ning, it is impossible to predict all the problems that are
likely to arise but here are some of the ways festival organisers deal with the unexpected.*

TAKING IT DAY BY DAY

You need to have a day plan of events so that you always know
what should be happening and where. This is very simple to
do but is absolutely invaluable in a crisis. Everyone involved
should be given a copy which has to include:

- day and date
- the venue name
- timings
- equipment details
- names of helpers
- the name of the host
- the names of people taking tickets
- anything else that is relevant to that particular event
- contact numbers for the people involved and that of the
  festival organiser

This means if someone drops out unexpectedly, a room host, perhaps, you know at once whom you can call on to step in.

DON'T BE OVERWHELMED BY THE UNEXPECTED

You will find there is so much going on in organising your festival, but you must be able to keep calm whatever unpredictable events hurtle your way. 'I think the most difficult thing is keeping a lot of plates spinning at the same time,' says Paul Kelly, of Bournemouth Jazz Festival. 'Inevitably, you are trying to liaise with the artists, you are trying to get the technical side sorted out, you are trying to sell all the tickets and you have to make sure you have all the permissions in place in time. There are a lot of different things to be juggling at the same time.'

Paul is right. You have to be prepared for many unlikely things to cause problems and this is one reason why running a festival can be physically and emotionally draining. The organiser has to be like a duck, serene on the surface but rushing about like mad underneath.

Lydia Brammer told me that lots of small issues came up as they were setting up the River Cottage Festival and they dealt with those as they came along. As the festival grew with longer hours and more people on site, they found they had to work on traffic management and security.

Sometimes you really can't predict what could go wrong even if your planning is exceptional, as Miles Halton relates. 'The worst happened last year. Most of the traders bring their own gazebos but we also put up marquees for them. The traders are inside and the punters are outside. They are also divided by internal walls and these free-standing marquees have a brace at one end. What I hadn't realised was that someone had decided the brace was in the way so they took it off! What happened was that the person next to them had noticed this and wanted to do the same. Luckily, she was quite a small person and had enlisted some help to take it off just as I was walking past. So we were just a couple of minutes from the whole marquee falling on a lot of people! It was a very nasty moment.'

Paula Prince had several nasty moments but usually managed to turn them to her advantage. 'We invited John Bird, who founded *The Big Issue*, to come and talk but it was at the last minute,' she explains. 'I knew I needed to publicise it so I made a figure like a Guy Fawkes, wearing my old clothes stuffed with polythene. I put him by the bookshop, lying on a blanket with his back to the street. All the way round this figure were statistics of homelessness in this county, even how many people were homeless in Oundle itself.

'I put a tin plate by him and well, people thought he was real! They put money in the tin plate and brought cakes for him and then someone told the police. Along they came and I get called out and discovered they were going to do me for breach of the peace! But that did me a lot of good, really, because the local television picked it up and we got a lot of publicity and John Bird's event packed the church!'

LEARNING BY EXPERIENCE

The first festival is always the hardest because you never know how popular it will be – even if you are experienced in organising events.

'One of the reasons we started the Great Dorset Chilli Festival was that I had been in the events business for a long time and it was a bit of a personal challenge for me to see whether I could apply my skills to a completely different sort of event,' Miles Halton explains. 'The main difficulty was knowing how popular it was going to be. There is a considerable amount of investment into an event this size and I needed to be sure I was going to get a return on that. The first year, marketing was very good. Because of my background, I knew I had to make the public fully aware of what was going on. I had no way of knowing how many people would come and in the end it was very popular but there wasn't quite enough happening. At that first festival there weren't enough stands and there wasn't enough to do. So there was a bit of criticism because the queues were too long and people sold out of their chilli sauces. That was the hardest learning curve for me. The second year we made all the changes and invested more into the whole event because we knew it was popular. The numbers were about the same as the first year and then in the third year it went crazy and we doubled our numbers.'

> Make sure there are enough attractions to keep everyone busy.

Janet Gleeson has had to deal with unhappy people – 'Grumpy volunteers are the most difficult!' she says. 'You do need a lot of help when the events are running. You need help in stewarding, taking tickets, manning the front desk, that kind of thing. There was a great response when we put out a call for help. We asked volunteers to tell us the times they were available to help but if they didn't get exactly the times and days they wanted some of them got quite grumpy, which was difficult. Now we're wised up to that and have appointed two people to focus completely on the volunteers and deal with briefing them. It was not easy to do all that as well as everything else.'

'In twenty-six years there were bound to be problems,' admits James Shepard, 'but the worst was when there was that big outbreak of foot-and-mouth disease [in 2001] and all agricultural shows were cancelled. We were lucky because it didn't actually happen near us but there were a lot of sleepless nights before we knew we were safe.'

Paul Kelly was faced with the loss of a top musician. 'If you've got good planning there probably isn't a problem,' he says, 'but the main objective is to get everything to the right place at the right time. I am meticulous in having lots of bits of paper that show exactly what should be happening and when. You need the schedule but the next big problem is when things don't go to plan. We had just launched the jazz festival with Ginger Baker, a rock drummer from the 1960s who is quite well known because he started a band called Cream with Eric Clapton. He is essentially a jazz drummer and he has gone back to playing jazz, and so we booked him as a headliner for the festival. We were getting quite a lot interest and then suddenly he found he had major heart problems and was going to have to have heart surgery and so he pulled out. That left us very little time to find a suitable replacement and that was a challenge.'

Always try and have substitutes available at short notice.

Luke Hasell of Valley Fest admits that starting a festival *is* a learning curve. 'We learnt a lot last year about the benefits of having a main stage as a focal point for the festival,' he says, 'as well as keeping everything in a smaller space to create a buzz for the festival-goers. Hopefully this year we'll have some new learnings!'

WHAT TO DO DO IF AN ACT LETS YOU DOWN

What you can do if you're left in the lurch rather depends on whether your guest is a no-show on the day or you are given some notice. With some notice, even if it is just a week, there is a chance you can find a replacement. You don't want to have to refund money for the tickets you have sold.

We had an event involving all the local book clubs. They were given the same book to read and we invited the author to come and discuss it with them. On the appointed day the author was ill and we were faced with having to refund ticket money. It seemed a better idea to carry on with the event and hold a discussion about the book amongst ourselves, offering to give back ticket money to anyone who felt they were losing out. Only three people opted to have their money returned and the event went well, probably better than if the author was there because people felt free to talk about what they disliked about the book.

You could try to find someone who is free to do a similar thing – flower-arranging should be fairly easy to replace, making scarecrows a bit trickier; bands are hardly in short supply and many would be pleased to be offered a gig (it's your decision whether you pay them the same fee as the original band but in all cases, make sure you give the audience the opportunity to have a refund).

POOR TICKET SALES

This shouldn't happen if you have been keeping an eye on movement. If sales are low a week before the event, increase your publicity. Usually, a local radio station will help, but if you do get to the point where no more tickets have been sold and you have fewer than ten people booked, there are two choices. Either you cancel the event or change it.

I heard about one speaker who had just seven people in his audience. To make matters worse, they were in a hall that had the capacity for over three hundred people. What the organisers should have done was find a smaller hall or try to use a library or a bookshop, serve tea or coffee and cake or biscuits and make it into an intimate gathering. Most bookshops have space where they can hold a talk and it is always sensible to have your local library involved if you are a literary festival.

TECHNICAL PROBLEMS

Make sure you have a technician on hand at all times to deal with the sound system and other electronic equipment. This will undoubtedly have an unfortunate habit of not working at vital times. Always check the sound system for each act before they are due on stage. This makes you feel comfortable and the act feel confident.

Paul Kelly spent seven years teaching people how to stage events. 'One of the things I found the students were not very good at was lighting,' he says. 'Lighting can make or break an event. If you want to create an atmosphere then get the lighting sorted out. The lighting and sound are both important as that is what can create the magic.'

SUMMARY

- A realistic day plan will avert potential disasters
- Be ready to make last-minute changes if an act lets you down or few tickets are sold
- Be aware that there can be technical problems at the last minute so make sure all the equipment needed for a performance is tested ahead of time.
- Remember that your first festival could be a stressful learning curve but the second will be much easier

10
Let the festival begin

You have done all the preparation; authors, musicians, stallholders or speakers are confirmed; the stage is dressed; the chairs in place and tickets sold. Everything is ready. Even so, it doesn't alter the fact that the first day can be incredibly stressful.

THE FIRST DAY

You will have a list of all your helpers clutched firmly in your hand: someone is selling tickets at the event, two people are taking tickets from members of the audience as they go into the hall. Your event's host, the people who introduce and thank the speaker, perhaps a bookseller with the speaker's current book and copies of previous books, hardbacks and paperbacks, are all ready. This is important because it means that people can buy books as they go in to the event as well as at the end. The green room is overflowing with wine, tea and coffee-makers, water – still and sparkling – a selection of biscuits and fresh flowers.

Stallholders have their spaces and people are on hand to direct them. Musicians have arrived and know their pitch. You and your team will be at the venue at least an hour before everyone else so that if there are any questions you can deal with them before the audience starts coming in.

> Remember some people will arrive very early and others just before the event starts.

Audiences always start to arrive early. It seems to be a fact of festival life. Be prepared for that and decide in advance whether you will let them in or make them wait. Have a couple of volunteers at the gate in good time. It helps to have seats around where people can sit while they are waiting.

Are you prepared?

Make sure you have an Emergency Box that contains:

- Scotch tape in two widths – two inches and one inch
- Scissors
- Felt pens
- Ballpoint pens
- A4 sheets of paper and card
- Drawing pins
- Blu-Tack
- Paperclips and bulldog clips
- Schedule of the day's events with times, helpers, chaperones, etc.
- Black bin bags
- Copies of the programme

You also need hot coffee and tea available for your volunteers throughout the day.

Have you put out rubbish bins in strategic places? There should be a volunteer on hand to check these regularly. Make sure there are bins handy where refreshments are sold.

Are there enough signs showing people where events are being held?

What about parking? Are the signs in place directing cars? Do you have at least two people ensuring that drivers park their cars tidily and sensibly?

Keep track of time

I have learnt from painful experience that it is not always wise to have a high-profile speaker for your first event. One speaker at our festival arrived twenty-five minutes late and spent another twenty-five minutes organising pull-up banners on the stage. This involved reorganising much of the stage furniture. Although we allow one hour before an event, that left about ten minutes before the talk was due to begin and people were arriving at least forty-five minutes early to secure a good seat. With all the moving backwards and forwards of stage furniture and changing the order of the pull-up banners, we couldn't let the audience into the hall and the queue outside grew and grew. We were expecting over two hundred people and they were getting very cross. Two of us were walking up and down the queue, apologising profusely. It didn't work; the audience was getting noisily frustrated. We should have numbered the tickets so people would have known where they were sitting and not arrived so early that they had to queue. You learn by experience.

Because this speaker had upset animal-rights organisations at an event a few days earlier, I had notified the police and had a security man on guard. The last thing we needed was a demonstration outside the hall. No demonstrators turned up which was a great relief. We had enough problems.

At last everything was ready, the audience, very disgruntled, filed in and the talk began. It went on and on and *on* and, despite the fact this person had personal charm, the talk was not hugely stimulating. Some people left, which may have been because they had other things to do, at which point the speaker said, very loudly, 'Am I boring you?' We usually allowed an hour for an event with the talk lasting twenty-five minutes, questions lasting fifteen minutes and the rest of the time for book signing. *This* talk went on for the whole hour and more, so we dispensed with questions and went straight to signing.

This is *not* the sort of event anyone wants at the start of a festival and we learnt a salutary lesson; start with someone who is well known for their timekeeping and gives amusing, informative or inspirational talks. Make sure the speaker knows how long he or she is expected to talk. One festival I went to had someone at the back of the hall with large pieces of card marked '15 minutes', '10 minutes', 'only 5 minutes'. That seemed to work. Or you could have a large clock, easily read from the stage. Do make sure the speakers, demonstrators or musicians know for how long they are expected to be on stage. Ask them if they would like you to give them a sign when they should be coming to an end of the session. Bear in mind, though, that they may ignore this completely.

THE EVENT HOST

I was at one festival when a speaker became totally carried away with the subject. The only way the event host could stop him was to make frantic circular movements with his arm at the back of the hall indicating 'Wind it up'. That worked. The event host will make sure that everything is in place before an event. Below are suggested guidelines that were designed for literary festivals but can be adapted easily for any festival. Give a copy of the guidelines to each event host and go through it with them making sure they fully understand what they have to do.

Guidelines for event hosts

Your main role is to make sure the event runs smoothly and this is a general guide to tasks roughly in order of priority.

- Arrive at the location where the event is taking place at least half an hour beforehand.
- Check chairs are in place. Make sure there is a table, chair and carafe of water on stage for the speaker/ demonstrator.
- Make sure that the ticket collectors are ready at the door.
- Check the sound system and make sure the speaker/ demonstrator is wired up and that the roaming mic is available.
- Start the proceedings on the dot!
- Welcome the audience and explain where the emergency exits are.
- Thank the sponsors of the event.
- Say you are going to hand over to the person introducing the speaker.
- When the speaker/demonstrator has finished, announce there is time for questions and operate the roving mic.
- Don't let the questions go on too long. Hand over to the person doing the thanks.

- Tell people that books or CDs are on sale and introduce any bookseller.
- Discourage long conversations between guest and customer tactfully.
- Don't let people wait around in the hall too long, and usher them out. Another event is usually about to take place.
- Make sure the room is tidy, the chairs are back in place and everything is ready for the next event when you leave.

Warning! Stay in the room where the event is taking place for the whole time. I was at an event at which the speaker had trouble with her microphone and there was no host to help her. The same speaker had to leave the stage to ask nearby workmen to be quiet as she was giving a talk. How embarrassing for the festival organisers! This sort of thing should never happen! It shows sloppy planning.

NEEDS AN INTRODUCTION

The person introducing the speaker/demonstrator must know something about that person, so if it's you, do your homework. The introduction should be brief and act as a welcome. I have known some people take at least fifteen minutes. Remember, the audience has come to hear the speaker, listen to the band or watch the demonstrator and not you! It is important to get your facts correct. I remember one person introducing a famous crime writer and announced the author had killed off his main sleuth when he hadn't! Very embarrassing. Here are some guidelines to hand to the people who have volunteered to introduce or thank a speaker or performer.

Guidelines for introductions

The introduction is very important because it sets the scene so here are a few things to remember:

- Research your guest – you will find that on the inside back flap of a book jacket, for example, there is usually a short biography, but you may want more.
- Familiarise yourself with the book/CD. You don't have to read it/listen to it all but get a flavour of the style.
- Arrive at the event at least half an hour before the start and meet your guest in the green room.
- Begin your introduction by saying how delighted you are the guest can join you.
- Say something about their background and career.
- Say a bit about the style – musical or writing or whatever – of the guest.
- Don't forget to mention questions if the audience will be invited to quiz the guest.
- Don't forget to mention opportunities for the audience to meet the guest afterwards and get product signed.
- Your introduction should take no more than *two minutes*.
- Do not mention buying books on Amazon at a literary festival if your bookseller is present.

When the speaker/demonstrator has finished and the questions have been answered, it is time to offer thanks. Again, this should be brief and involve something the speaker/demonstrator has said or shown (so everyone knows you have been watching and listening). See the following guidelines:

Guidelines for thanks

- During the event, jot down the occasional note as you might like to include a comment in your thanks. This is just a suggestion and not an instruction!
- Simply thank the guest for a really interesting experience, say how much you and everyone else has enjoyed it.
- Alternatively, give a fascinating, inspirational, previously prepared vote of thanks of your own!
- Remind everyone of any after-show signing.
- Only take a couple of minutes – no more than two or three minutes maximum.

KEEPING TIME

It is vital you keep to the timings allotted to the event or you will find everything runs late and you have angry audiences and, worse, an angry speaker.

No event should last longer than an hour and that should include the introduction, the talk, the questions, the thanks and the book-signing. A book signing can overrun and it helps if it can be done outside the hall – which may well need to be prepared for the next event.

FEEDBACK

Conduct a survey

Although you will have picked up the vibes on how your event went it is useful to have some more formal feedback. You need to know how the audience enjoyed themselves and, very importantly, their comments, good and bad. You can leave a list of questions on seats, hand them out as the audience leaves or designate an interviewer to ask people after the event. I recommend the latter because it gives you more control. It is important to have a cross-section of the audience and not just, say, women of the same age group who will usually have similar views. You have no control over this if you leave questions on seats. People don't mind being asked questions (it makes them feel important, which they are) as long as there are not too many and it does not take more than a few minutes.

- Before you ask these questions, write the date and the event at the top of the sheet.
- Try to get as wide an age range as possible and ask as many people leaving the event as you can.
- It is worth having two or three people involved in asking the questions.
- Be aware that if it is a late-night event, nobody will want to hang around answering questions.

Tailor your questions carefully:

1 Are you enjoying the festival? Yes/no – if no, why not?
2 How did you hear about the festival?
3 Which events have you seen/heard?
4 Did you have problems buying tickets?
5 Where did you get them? Internet? Ticket sellers? Box office?
6 Do you think the ticket price was value for money? – if not, why?
7 How could we improve the festival?

8 How likely are you to attend this festival next year?

9 Would you recommend the festival to you friends?

10 Where do you live?

11 How did you travel to the festival?

12 Are you staying in the town?

13 Which age group do you fall into? 16-21; 22-45; 46-65; 65+

Don't make your questionnaire any longer because collating the answers takes up too much time. It's going to be particularly interesting to see where people come from, how they travelled and if they are staying locally. That will help your advertising and publicity next year. The age group is also significant – you can see whether your audience consists mainly of older or younger people or a mixture and that will help you focus your programming for future events. Analysing the questionnaires is a bit of a chore but definitely worth the time and effort.

If you follow the advice in this chapter you should – with a bit of luck – have a smooth start to your festival. Do make sure everyone on your team has a few breaks during the day. You all need to be able to sit down, have a sandwich or a bowl of soup, do a crossword or knit – in other words, forget about the festival for an hour (if possible) and clear your head.

SUMMARY

- Festival-goers tend to arrive early so be prepared
- Keep the Emergency Box to hand
- Make sure guests start and finish on time – the event host should be the enforcer

- Introductions and thanks are important. People chosen to make these should do their research
- A simple survey is an invaluable tool to tell you what festival-goers like and dislike

11

Improving, enhancing, refining

After your first festival you will heave a sigh of relief and it's worth waiting a week to let everything settle before having a debriefing (a 'wash-up'). If you have surveyed your audience and analysed the questionnaires (see previous chapter) that will give you a valuable insight into how the festival was received by the audiences, what they liked and what they disliked and how far they travelled.

As you prepare to grow your festival you should take on board some wise advice from Tim Barford. 'There is no easy way so you are going to learn the hard way. It probably helps to start relatively small. It's a balance. On one hand you don't want to be afraid to do stuff but on the other hand you don't want to bite off too much and then perhaps fall flat. You learn from each festival. Some people won't be happy but they may make a good point and you should listen them. It's tough but listen to all the comments, good and bad, because they could improve your festival.'

MAKING IMPROVEMENTS FOR NEXT YEAR

What can you do to improve things next year? Perhaps you need to find more helpers, to change some of the timings or to add more evening events. Having done your first festival you will be much more confident when you are organising the next one and feel ready to let it start to grow. This is where the feedback from the questionnaires will come in very useful.

Could you add an extra day?

It would not be wise to suddenly hold a two-week festival when you have only had the experience of holding one at the weekend but to add an extra day or two would be feasible.

How can you improve?

Look at your children's events. Decide whether there are enough and whether these are events to appeal to children of all ages. Children love variety and doing things.

Could you have a corner for the kids?

A properly supervised crèche is very popular with mums and dads who will happily pay for the privilege of being on their own for a while and enjoying the festival.

Can you pop up with a pop-up?

A pop-up café would provide a haven for a cup of coffee or a light meal between events. This is an ideal meeting place, too.

Look into the health and safety hygiene regulations because you must have at least one qualified person in charge of a kitchen, but that qualification is easy to get online.

Make it simple. Borrow or hire an easy-to-operate coffee machine. Unless you are an expert, don't attempt to make fancy coffees. Offer different teas and soft drinks and, if you have a licence, a glass of wine. Home-made cakes and scones go down a treat and make sure you always have some interesting biscuits. The light meals should be simple and include homemade soups and sandwiches, and jacket potatoes if you have an oven handy. Try and be creative with ploughman's platters.

Of course, this is assuming you have a kitchen to hand. If not, it is possible to hire a variety of equipment such as a six-burner range cooker and oven that usually comes with Calor gas bottles; a hot cupboard; a potato baker or pizza cooker; and even a refrigerated trailer. Water can be tricky but a hose-pipe connected to a fairly distant tap usually works.

If you're reading this before you've done your first festival, don't be overambitious and do keep hire equipment to a minimum.

PICK AND MIX IDEAS

If you've been inspired by some of the events you've read about in this book, feel free to adapt them yourself as your festival develops. You may remember we decided to do 'Poems in a Pub with a Pint'. We sold the idea to a local landlord and chose a night when it was not too busy. A couple of hours is usually about the right length of time and as long as the potential poets buy a pint, a glass of wine or an orange juice the landlord is happy. Have a couple of festival people there and you are likely to have a fascinating evening. Suddenly there are people you have never seen before with poems they have written or particularly enjoy. Then there was our festival church service. For us it was a literary service and we had an enthusiastic vicar who came up with a huge number of literary references in the Bible and chose hymns written by well-known poets. You could adapt this with a musical theme or food. There are many mentions of food in the Bible and it is fun to put together a service using these references.

Talk to your local library and try to find a connection to your festival that you can use to your advantage. As we discovered earlier, Fringe in the Fen festival has Lancelot 'Capability' Brown buried in the village, while Dorchester homed in on Thomas Hardy and T. E. Lawrence. Or you may have a site that you want to expand without losing its identity. This is something that appeals to Luke Hasell: 'We'd love to grow Valley Fest to reach the site capacity of five thousand but keep it really boutique and true to its uncommercial roots,' he told me.

Kenneth Richardson's International Music Festival took over other events in the town and expanded the remit of the festival. 'We now run the Oundle Food Festival which is a one-day event and is incorporated into the music festival,' he says. 'On one of the Saturdays in the festival we shut down the centre of Oundle and have about seventy or eighty food stalls with producers of interesting foods that come from the local area – Lincolnshire, Leicestershire, Northamptonshire and Cambridgeshire. We have Music in Special Places and an autumn and spring concert series with folk, jazz and classical music. We also run a community-based cinema. There is a lot of activity and we have a hub for lots of organisations and have built up a database of people. We introduced an outdoor cinema in a big field on the edge of the town and people bring their deck chairs and their picnics. We get about three hundred people but, of course, it is weather dependent. All this is helping the town by boosting the economy.'

Don't worry if that seems like a lot of suggestions – you shouldn't make too many changes at once anyway. In any case, even a simple idea can improve or enhance a festival. At Sidmouth they included a fast-food stall selling ice creams and hot dogs that proved very popular.

CALL IN THE EXPERTS

Diana Cambridge is an experienced agony aunt – for writers. She is an author herself, runs writing workshops both face to face and online, and is an inspirational tutor. She writes about the work of a writer-in-residence and gives practical tips based on her three years working with a literary festival. All her advice can easily be adapted to benefit a whole range of themes.

Using a writer-in-residence

A writer-in-residence can add prestige, drive traffic to the site, publicise the organisation and improve facilities by adding a free or inexpensive extra service. But if you're doing the hiring, take care. Apart from selecting someone with a rock-solid professional background, your candidate needs lashings of tact combined with the ability to give usable, practical advice. What you don't want is someone who may upset

fledgling writers – or someone who offers unrealistic expect-
ations. It's a juggling act.

I was writer-in-residence at a literary festival from 2013 to
2015. This was a five-day event, and I set up both an advance
bookings system (with writers emailing me a work sample in
advance so I had a written critique ready to give them) and a
daily drop-in clinic.

I'd decided early on that no one would be turned away, and
the original hours of the writing clinic could be extended
without difficulty to the end of the day. I had to make sure the
booked writers were seen at the times they wanted – and
fitted all the drop-ins around them.

I preferred to stay in the town the whole time. If you are
looking for a writer-in-residence, you'll get better value that
way and reliability – but to keep your budget on track you
may have to provide accommodation. It's best if someone in
your organisation has a room with a desk and, hopefully, an
en-suite that they will happily provide for your writer (who
will be out most of the time, and shouldn't require any meals).

Drop-ins

Writers dropping in are as important as bookings – the writing clinic must be open to all. If the writer-in-residence can
offer a drop-in clinic at your festival, it's a definite asset, in my
view. New writers often have fragile egos, and may not decide
until the day whether they feel strong enough to have their
work examined.

My service was first offered as a free one and most users
also booked for events (which included talks by Kate Adie,
Joanna Trollope and Tracey Chevalier) and if they were not
local also spent money at the café, B&Bs and shops. In the

third year, a charge was made to writers and though this was small – five pounds – I noticed that numbers dropped.

Each writer had at least twenty minutes with me, plus a written critique and practical advice to take their work forward. I took lists of books and tip sheets to give to each writer. If I only saw their writing for the first time on the day, I could still do a basic critique. Having worked as a daily newspaper journalist for thirty years, I was used to rapid evaluation of words. This is another skill you as festival organiser might look for.

Sandwiching comments

I believe that if writers have bothered to show you their work and come along to see you, it already shows they take their writing seriously. Where there are problems, nine times out of ten these will be in structure and plot, not use of words. Introductions and endings are particular obstacles for new writers.

The writer-in-residence should make a 'sandwich' of her comments. He or she needs to find encouraging things to say at the beginning. For example, I'm always impressed if a writer has actually completed a piece of work, be it a novel, a story or a play. Thousands of would-be writers have abandoned projects tucked away all over their houses! The ability to finish is admirable. Where your expert can suggest improvements – and these are generally to structure and length (most new writers overwrite) they must stress that these are *suggestions*, not dictates! I usually offered firm, sometimes even surgical, professional advice, but made it clear that it was up to the student to follow this, or not. This advice was the 'meat' of the sandwich.

Will the writer ask your students for their views on what she's just said?

Does the work make sense to them?

They are working together – it's not a question of teacher and pupil.

In the third part of the sandwich, the expert can sum up the ways of moving on and perhaps offer an email follow-up. This should be free, I think. How much pro bono work you do is your decision. Personally, I'm keen on goodwill.

Advance booking

When writers have booked for my residency, I ask for a work sample to be sent ahead and adjust this in advance. A few tweaks – and deletions – can improve the content hugely, without changing the writer's vision. Almost always work is improved significantly by cutting – for example, the first chapter, the first few paragraphs and any sentimental, convenient or too-tragic endings.

It's important to try not to keep anyone waiting too long – it's easy for someone who has already taken the step of booking to see you to lose confidence if they're kept waiting. If it's inevitable, at least the writer-in-residence might pop out to say, 'Hello' and to explain the short wait. This is where some pre-planning by the festival organisers will help. The expert may need someone to be a gatekeeper.

How much should you pay your writer-in-residence?

Base the fee on what you are paying the speakers. But don't forget the residency is excellent publicity for the expert. If you provide free lunch, free accommodation and free tickets that's a great bonus.

How the writer-in-residence can help

- Keep tweeting even if you're very busy.
- Make sure you tweet if you have spaces left on any workshops you're doing.
- Do try to drop in on the sponsors just to say 'Hello'.
- Take photographs to post on your website (if students agree). It's easy to become absorbed by your work and forget these wider aspects that can be helpful to you.
- Go to as many events yourself as you can – most festivals will give free passes to their writer-in-residence.
- If you want to be available to everyone at the festival, you need to wear a badge.
- Ensure the festival put you and your picture in the programme.
- Prepare some posters to put up on the doors of rooms where you'll be based.
- Do all you can ahead of the festival to reduce the work being done by the doubtless overloaded festival helpers.
- Be well supplied with pens, paper, etc.

Recruiting a writer-in-residence

- Has he or she a website? On social media?
- Is she or he able to read and evaluate work quickly?
- If he or she has had any books published, especially how-to writing books, will he or she bring some along?
- Is she or he willing to give extra writing workshops and include them in the residency?

Useful skills for a writer-in-residence

A City & Guilds PTTLLS (Preparation to Teach in the Lifelong Learning Sector) certificate can be gained at evening classes at a city college in three months or so. This includes two micro-teaches and you pick up modern strategies for teaching and helping students. You need to be interviewed and considered for the course, attend classes and give presentations, produce a portfolio and do teaching sessions which are assessed by the course presenter. I found gaining this certificate invaluable. Of course, if a writer-in-residence already has creative-writing teaching experience in a college that's a huge plus.

Any kind of coaching or mentoring courses will be helpful to a writer-in-residence, although the role isn't counselling but rather conveying practical advice as well as encouragement. Merely sympathising with a writer's lack of motivation doesn't help them: the expert's job is to animate them and move them on. They should leave the session looking forward to working on their next writing project.

Practicalities for the festival

- Comfortable but good shoes – essential!
- Drink plenty of water – keep a bottle by you during the day.
- Remember to eat – the festival you're working for will often include free lunch at their café.
- Try and get at least ten minutes of fresh air every day.
- Prepare to be away from the rest of the festival team for a few hours while you're seeing writers, and mostly to lunch alone – if you're someone who'd feel lonely, a writer-in-residence role may not be for you.

145

- Keep all your equipment together – you may have to move around the building as different spaces become occupied by visiting authors or workshops. Do be flexible about this and have a roomy bag with compartments to keep all your papers.

If your festival is not a literary one, you can still have a resident expert! Adjust all the above pointers towards your festival – you could have a resident musician, chef, wine buff or guru in any discipline. You need someone who will see visitors who want to discuss their own music, food, garden or whatever will be a draw.

SUMMARY

- Expand gradually by adding just a few extra events or an extra day each year
- Make the festival more appealing for adults by including more children's events or a crèche
- Think about starting a pop-up café; otherwise, try and have hot and cold drinks available
- Have an expert on hand – a writer-in-residence, a musician, a chef demonstrating his or her skills or a guru whose expertise reflects your festival

Afterword

It's over! The marquees are taken down, the permanent venues emptied, the rubbish bags taken to the rubbish tip, the last visitor has left – and that's it! How do you feel? Elated because nothing too terrible went wrong? Exhausted because you haven't stopped talking and dealing with queries and welcoming and saying 'Goodbye' to people? It's probably a bit of everything but maybe you just feel relieved that it's all over and life can get back to normal.

There are still a few things you need to do. In a couple of weeks' time and no earlier because you want everything to settle in your head, gather your team together for a 'wash-up'. You need to talk about the festival honestly and objectively and discuss how it could be improved, the things that were successful and those you would not do again. Be careful not to blame others: everyone can make a mistake and this is not a time for recriminations.

Write short but warm thank-you notes, emails or even texts to everyone! It's a chore, I know, but they will be much appreciated by the recipients and next year they will remember! Send thank-yous not only to the people taking part and their agents or publicists but to most people who have been involved, not forgetting the venue caretaker. Remember, too, the advertisers and sponsors, the local newspapers and the monthly magazines that gave you good coverage. It can be a big task if you do it properly but it is not something that only one person has to do. You can always get a couple of your team to help.

On the subject of help, give a party for the helpers! You could use one of your venues although that will mean you producing wine and nibbles but the idea is just to get everyone together and say a public thank-you. You may prefer to arrange something with a local pub that will cost a bit more but will take the pressure off you. If your treasurer has completed the accounts it is always good to give people who have been involved advance information on the amount of money made and what you plan to do with the profits. Will they go to charity or will you invest them back into the festival? Maybe a bit of each. Remember you need your start-up money for next year's events.

Finally, take yourself and your committee or team out to a special lunch or dinner to celebrate your success. You deserve it!

Appendix I
Contract and
information sheet

A letter of contract and information sheet means that everyone knows what has been agreed between the festival organiser and the performer and agents. When agreements are made several months ahead, it is easy to forget some of the details. This is a simple draft contract for an author but it is easily adapted for any speaker or demonstrator. Send *two* copies so that one can be returned to you and if there is any query you can refer to it. Include a stamped addressed envelope.

CONTRACT LETTER

To (name)

Date

Dear (name)

(Name of festival) (year)

I am writing to thank you very much for agreeing to take part in the (year and name of festival). I would be grateful if you could sign one copy of this letter and return it to me along with a completed information sheet as soon as possible. This will give us all the practical details we need to make sure your event runs smoothly.

Date:
Length of time of event:
Your event: please let us know by the beginning of [state month] what props you need for your event. We have microphones that clip onto a collar as well as hand-held and fixed. We usually dress the stage with an armchair, table, standard lamp, bookcase etc. and we can leave these ready for you or clear them away. We also provide a carafe of water [adapt as necessary].

Accommodation: the festival will book and pay for a double room for you and your wife for the night of . . . . If your accommodation plans change I would be grateful if you could let me know by (date).

Please note all sundry expenses including room service, telephone calls or bar bills must be settled personally on your departure from the hotel.

Arrival: when you arrive please check in at . . . . where a member of the festival team will meet you.

Arrangements for the event: we would like you to arrive at the hall one hour before the event, i.e. . . . . A member of the festival team will collect you from the hotel at . . . . We would like you to do a sound test and check everything is in order before your event. [adapt as necessary]

Hospitality: we like to look after our guests and a selection of hot and cold drinks and snacks will be available in the green room. If we have agreed to give you a meal before/

after your event, we will pay for the food but not for any alcoholic drinks; that will be your responsibility.

Bookselling [or other merchandising as appropriate]: your books will be on sale in the town before and after the event. On the day, they will be on sale in the hall and we would like you to take the opportunity to sign copies bought by the audience.

Our festival book seller is, (name), (address)

Please would you pass these details to your publisher?

Publicity: we will do our best to publicise your event widely in the media. Please let us have a short biography (max. two hundred words), and a digital photograph (300 dpi) of yourself and the latest book jacket as soon as possible. Could you also give us the title of your talk.

Fee: we have agreed a fee with you of £XX and a cheque for this amount will be paid after your appearance and on receipt of your invoice. If you are VAT-registered we will require a VAT invoice before payment can be made.

Insurance cover: the festival undertakes responsibility for fire, public, third-party and employer's liability cover in respect of the venue, venue staff, and the general public visiting the venue. It is your responsibility to be insured against the loss or theft of equipment and personal possessions; the festival can take no responsibility for any such loss.

Other events: Please let us know if you will be appearing at any other literary festivals in this area within a month either side of this festival.

Please sign one copy of this letter of agreement and return it together with a completed information sheet to me at the address below as soon as possible.

If you have any queries regarding your event please do

not hesitate to contact the festival organiser, (your name), on: (telephone number) or email (email address).

We very much look forward to welcoming you.

Yours sincerely

I understand and agree to the terms outlined above

Signature: _____ Date: _____

Please return one copy of this letter and your information sheet to . . . .

You will note that the contract stipulates that if the festival agrees to pay for a meal, it does not agree to pay for any alcohol consumed. The reason for this is that one year we had our fingers badly burnt. We had agreed to pay for a meal for one author and we discovered this author had ordered a bottle of wine costing £64 to go with it! That was a bit naughty because we were already giving him extra money negotiated by his agent.

It helps everyone if you include an information sheet with the contract. The information sheet is important because it tells you what the author or demonstrator needs. Having the contract and the information sheet saves confusion.

INFORMATION SHEET

Thank you for agreeing to appear at the Festival. It would be a great help to us if you could confirm your contact details and let us know your plans as early as possible to avoid any disappointment and to aid our planning.

In order to do so, please complete this form and return by (date) to (your name) the festival secretary.

Contact details

Full address: . . . .
. . . .
. . . .
. . . .

Mobile number (for emergency contact during the festival only): . . . .

Travel arrangements

I will be departing from . . . . (city/town)
I will be arriving by road / rail* on . . . . (date)
(*please delete as applicable)
I will arrive at . . . . (time)

Arrangements for the festival

☐ I require DVD/ video projection (please state standard: PAL, NTSC)
☐ I require PowerPoint projection with/without* a laptop (*please delete as applicable)
☐ I require CD/MP3 audio equipment
Please list any other special requirements below:

. . . .
. . . .
. . . .
. . . .

Accommodation

I DO/DO NOT require accommodation for the night of (date).

If you would like to add extra nights to your stay, single rooms are £XX per room per night and double rooms are £XX per room per night, including English breakfast, services and VAT.

If you would like to upgrade your room to a double or twin room during your allocated night, the additional cost will be £XX per night.

Festival filming and recording

☐ I DO NOT wish my event(s) to be filmed or recorded.

Fee waiver

☐ I would like to support the festival by generously agreeing to waive my fee.

Participant signature: . . . .

Date: . . . .

To discuss your event, or any queries about your accommodation, please contact the festival secretary: (telephone number) or email (email address).

Appendix II

If you are hiring speakers, the Society of Authors issues a useful leaflet on what you have to remember. This is practical information and can be adapted to different events – music, food, arts – and people taking part: stallholders, refreshment trailers, children's events, etc.

ADVICE FROM THE SOCIETY OF AUTHORS

Authors are usually delighted to be invited to appear at festivals. The following information and checklist are provided in order to ensure author appearances are handled as smoothly and fairly as possible, in the interests of the author, the festival and the audience.

ENGAGING AN AUTHOR

When arranging your event all significant points should be confirmed in writing with the author, and (if relevant) their publisher or agent as soon as possible. Any points in relation to obligations or permissions (e.g. event recordings or publicity requirements) must be agreed at the time the author is first contacted. Festival organisers tell us they tend to receive a better response when communicating by email, as opposed to post. Authors vary in their approach and neither form is reliable so it can avoid later misunderstandings if you use both.

THE EVENT

Live performances can be nerve-racking enough, so the author will need to know all the particulars of the event itself well in advance. This goes beyond the obvious whens and wheres – the more the author knows about what to expect and how to prepare the more confident they will feel and the better your event will be. A little TLC goes a long way!

When

- the date of the event
- the time of the event
- the parallel events/sessions taking place (as this may affect audiences)

What

- the purpose and title of the event
- the length of the event
- the nature of the event (reading, talk, panel discussion), how much of this should be the author's presentation and how much a Q&A session

- how the author will be introduced/described (in both the event itself and any promotion)
- the programme's description of the event
- the event sponsor

Who

- whether there will be a chairperson and if so who they are and how they can be contacted
- the name and contact details of the organiser, including the details of a named person who can be contacted on the day
- who else is taking part, and if the author can or should contact them in advance
- the expected profile of the audience

Where

- the nature of the venue (staging, lighting, etc.)
- the availability of technical equipment and assistance in its use

RIGHTS AND LEGAL FORMALITIES

Recording events

If you wish to make a recording (or printed or podcast version) of the event, the author's permission must be obtained. To avoid misunderstanding and awkwardness, ensure you clarify your intentions and obtain permission at the outset. Authors may not be willing to agree, for a variety of reasons; it may inhibit how they talk or the presentation could be one they want to repeat.

Identification

Clarify in advance if and what ID you require from the author.

Public liability insurance

Ensure you inform the author if you require individuals to possess public liability insurance.

Exclusion areas

We have seen a worrying trend for festivals to demand that an author does not appear at another festival or event within a specified distance and time period – sometimes as much as three months. Such clauses should be avoided as they are unnecessary and unfair; there is no reason to believe other events have an impact on ticket sales and such restrictions may prevent an author from undertaking a tour. If you do wish to impose an exclusion clause then your fee should compensate the author in full for the lost opportunities.

BEFORE AND AFTER

When engaging an author it is important to consider the arrangements beyond the event itself. The author needs to know where they are going and when, how they will get there and (extremely important) who they are meeting. Contact details (emails and mobile numbers) should be exchanged and maps provided. Let the author know if they will need accommodation and who is responsible for booking accommodation and travel. Will they have a reserved parking space? Is there anything they should know about accessing the festival site?

Explain the arrangements for refreshments and where the author can relax or prepare before and after the event. Ask the author about any dietary requirements or disabilities of which you should be aware. Are they allowed to bring a partner or friend with them – or a dog? Is there wi-fi?

Who will be in control of the bookselling arrangements and supplying books? What do you require the author to bring? Can you photocopy materials if necessary?

What information will you want from the author in advance? Obtain their website address and social media handles, and details of latest and forthcoming books.

PAYMENT AND EXPENSES

Tax and National Insurance

When paying freelance authors, neither tax nor NI should be deducted. Most authors are self-employed (even where they invoice as a limited company) and a one-off engagement does not create a contract of employment.

VAT

Authors who are VAT-registered are legally obliged to charge VAT on top of both the fee and expenses.

Fees

The negotiation of fees is a matter for individuals. However, all festivals – especially those with commercial sponsors, and any festival where the public pays for tickets – should offer reasonable fees as a matter of course. Fees should take into account travel and preparation time as well as actual perform-ance time. They should also take into account the annual salary an author would expect to earn as a freelance. We recommend Andrew Bibby's reckoner, www.andrewbibby.com/reckoner.html, which shows daily rates to equate with different salaries. Using that reckoner, a fee of £100 equates to an annual salary of just £9000, or £150 to an annual salary of £13,500 (The NASUWT 2013 salaries for leading practi-tioners (excluding London and the Fringe) are from £37,836-£57,520, which would equate to a fee of around £400 to £600).

The author should be paid within 30 days of the event.

Expenses

Will it be you or the publisher who is paying the author's travel and subsistence expenses? Will they be paid in advance or arrears?

Invoice

Does the author need to supply an invoice? Assuming yes, does it need a reference number or other identifier? To whom, at what address, should the invoice be sent? Does the author need to supply receipts?

Cancellation

If the event is cancelled the author must be given notice. If the booking is conditional, this must be clarified at the outset and any cancellation fees and timings must be made clear. We suggest:

- The author must be paid in full if the event is cancelled within six weeks of the event date;
- The author must be paid fifty per cent if the event is cancelled earlier;
- Any out-of-pocket expenses already incurred must be reimbursed whenever the event is cancelled.

CHECKLIST FOR FESTIVAL ORGANISERS TO CONFIRM WITH THE AUTHOR

The following should be agreed in writing as far in advance of the event as possible

The date and time of event ☐

Location (site and precise venue) of event ☐

When you will require the author to arrive/be present. Can they stay for the rest of the festival? Are they welcome to attend other events? Do they need to book tickets? Are complimentary tickets available for companions, publicists or others? ☐

The nature of the venue (e.g. lecture theatre, informal circle) and any relevant features (e.g. poor lighting) ☐

The purpose and title of the event. Is it part of a strand of sessions within the festival programme? ☐

How will you introduce/describe the author in the
event and in any programme, promotion or publicity?
Biographical details are de facto personal and should
be approved by the author in each instance   ☐
The expected audience profile and size (e.g.
aspiring writers, reading group, general public).
What parallel sessions are taking place? (this can
affect attendance)   ☐
The nature of the session (reading, talk, panel
discussion)   ☐
Who is taking part in the event? Will the author be on
his/her own, and/or chaired, and/or with fellow
panellists? If so, who are they? Can/should the author
contact any of them in advance and, if so, how?   ☐
The number and length of the author's session(s) within
the event, and how much of any session should be a
presentation by the author and how much left for
questions and answers   ☐
The event sponsor(s)   ☐
The availability of technical equipment (projector,
PowerPoint, internet connection). Can the author
check the site before the talk? Can you provide someone to check that the equipment functions, and be on
site in case it fails? How far in advance will an author
need to provide you with any presentation materials?   ☐
Whether you wish to record the event, in what manner
(audio/audio-visual/transcription) and for what purpose
(podcast/website/monetisation). How will this be
compensated?   ☐
Whether the author will need public liability insurance   ☐
Whether the author needs to bring ID and in
what form   ☐

Who is meeting the author, when and where? ☐
Will the author need accommodation and who
will pay for and organise this? ☐
Who is responsible for booking travel tickets? ☐
Will a parking space be reserved for the author? ☐
What is the position if the author would like to bring/
travel with a partner – or a dog? ☐
What are the arrangements for refreshments?
Are these provided/reimbursed? ☐
Is the author obliged or welcome to stay for
refreshments or a meal with the audience or
other participants? ☐
Is there an area in which the author can relax/
prepare before and/or after the event? ☐
Is the author expected to bring support materials
e.g. a copy of their own book, or handouts? May they
do so if they wish? Can you photocopy materials if
needed? ☐
If you can offer authors the chance to sell their own
books, who will sort out the arrangements for supplying
books (generally the author or their publisher, sometimes a local bookshop)? Will someone (not the author)
be on hand to sell the books? ☐
What fees will be paid? ☐
Whether the payment of fees is taxable. When paying
freelance authors, neither tax nor NI should be
deducted. Most authors are self-employed (even where
they invoice as a limited company) and a one-off
engagement does not create a contract of employment ☐
Whether the author is VAT-registered. Authors who are
VAT-registered are legally obliged to charge VAT on top
of both the fee and expenses ☐

What expenses will be paid and by whom?
Will it be you or the publisher who is paying
the author's travel and subsistence expenses?
Does the author need to supply receipts? Will these
be paid in advance? ☐

When will the author be paid? It should be within
thirty days of the event ☐

Does the author need to supply an invoice? Where
should it be sent? Does it need a reference number
or other identifier? ☐

If the event is cancelled, how much notice will the
author be given? The author should be refunded any
expenses already incurred. If the author has had to turn
down other engagements, or is otherwise left out of
pocket e.g. because of a late cancellation, they should
be paid the full fee ☐

*Ensure you request the following from the author in a timely
manner. You may also have other information or items that
you require which are not listed here.*

- Contact details: email, landline phone, mobile phone, postal address
- Online information: website, blog, Twitter handle, Facebook page, etc.
- Details of latest and forthcoming books/projects
- Biographical information
- Contact details for their publisher/agent/publicist (if relevant)
- Next of kin details (in case of emergency)
- Details and requirements of any disabilities
- Any dietary requirements

The following should be provided for the author as far as possible in advance of the event.

- Names and contact details for the event organiser and the point of contact on the day, including emails and mobile phone numbers
- A map of how to reach the location of the festival site and information on public transport
- A map of the site itself

FINAL NOTES

The Society of Authors chief executive, Nicola Solomon, writes:

'The SOA believes authors should be properly paid for festivals and appearances because:

- A talk involves preparation and travelling time (so for the author an event will rarely take up less than a full working day in practice).
- Authors earn their living as freelances. If a festival is asking the author to give up a day of their time for professional purposes, it is only fair that time is paid for.
- Everyone else involved in providing services to the festival is being paid (we know that many festival organisers and helpers put in a huge amount of time but they are doing this as a hobby).
- If the festival is charging the public to attend, the author should be entitled to a share of the monies generated.
- The sponsors of big festivals are wealthy and they are demanding ever more from their speakers – authors should not feel that they are somehow being disloyal or unsupportive of the festival staff if they ask for a reasonable fee.

- The more the festival seeks to take, the better the author should be paid. For example, if the writer is being asked to allow their event to be recorded for public dissemination, they should be compensated appropriately in addition to their speaking fees.
- We strongly believe that payment in kind is not an acceptable alternative.'

Acknowledgements

I am indebted to Diana Cambridge, a friend and colleague, who helped me develop an embryo of an idea for this book and encouraged me to write it; Paul Kelly, who generously shared his vast experience and expertise; Tanya Bruce-Lockhart who made so many practical suggestions; Steve Heap of the Association of Festival Organisers who shared some of his vast experience in festival organisation; Jane Adkins, who has supported me throughout; and to all my many friends – authors and musicians in particular – who gave me so much valuable information, thank you.

I must thank all the festival organisers who explained how they ran their festivals and gave me such wonderful advice to pass on, and especially my editor, Nikki Read, for her clever suggestions and amazing patience, and Rebecca Sheppard and the rest of the team at Little, Brown. Finally, I must not forget Hamish, who insisted I left my desk and went out into the fresh air and for walks which helped me clarify my thoughts. I could not have written this book without you all!

Index